*Samuel French Acting Edition*

D0775405

# Theater Masters' Take Ten Volume III

*A Girl's Gotta Do, etc.*
Julia Izumi

*A Last Night on Earth*
Hannah Doran

*A Short Man and the Eyeballs*
Yi Hsuan Tseng

*Everything You'll Miss in Minutes*
Lauren Wimmer

*Reverse/Loop/Repeat*
Steph Del Rosso

*Ron Don Jon Juan*
Anna Fox

*Sink. Row. Nice!*
Marvin González De León

*Sway*
Kristen Field

SAMUELFRENCH.COM    SAMUELFRENCH.CO.UK

ISBN 978-0-573-70697-4

www.SamuelFrench.com
www.SamuelFrench.co.uk

### MUSIC USE NOTE

Licensees are solely responsible for obtaining formal written permission from copyright owners to use copyrighted music in the performance of this play and are strongly cautioned to do so. If no such permission is obtained by the licensee, then the licensee must use only original music that the licensee owns and controls. Licensees are solely responsible and liable for all music clearances and shall indemnify the copyright owners of the play(s) and their licensing agent, Samuel French, against any costs, expenses, losses and liabilities arising from the use of music by licensees. Please contact the appropriate music licensing authority in your territory for the rights to any incidental music.

### IMPORTANT BILLING AND CREDIT REQUIREMENTS

If you have obtained performance rights to this title, please refer to your licensing agreement for important billing and credit requirements.

# INTRODUCTION

Take Ten is our national ten-minute play competition for playwrights from some of the top MFA programs in the country. Each year six to ten playwrights are flown to Aspen, Colorado for a workshop production with a professional director and the local community of actors. In the spring, the playwrights and their directors travel to New York for an equity showcase production of these same plays. The program in many ways serves as an on-ramp for these MFA playwrights from the academic to the professional theater community. Our programming arms these young artists for the industry and offers them a platform to share their unique voices with the American Theater.

Take Ten is our effort to launch new and exciting voices into the American Theater by taking writers from some of the top MFA programs around the country and giving them a platform to introduce themselves and share their unique voices with the New York Theater community.

Julia Hansen founded the National MFA Playwrights Competition and Take Ten Festival in 2007 when she saw a need for an organization to bridge the gap between the training playwrights were receiving and the professional careers that lay ahead of them. Take Ten's dual-leg professional development opportunity, as well as this partnership with Samuel French, provide playwrights a career-igniting entrance into the entertainment industry and introduce their work to the American Theater.

We are grateful to all who have supported us – the schools who include us in their programs (Arizona State University, Brown, Carnegie Mellon, Columbia, Fordham/Primary Stages, Northwestern, NYU, University of Iowa, University of Texas at Austin, UCLA, UCSD, and Yale School of Drama); individuals through financial and in-kind donations; our professional artists through their diligence and hard work; and our board for making this program possible and dreams come true for our playwrights.

We are pleased to now share with you the third anthology of Theater Masters' plays, those presented in our 2017 National MFA Playwrights Festival.

Sincerely,

Joseph Ward
Executive Artistic Director

# TABLE OF CONTENTS

# A Girl's Gotta Do, etc.

### Julia Izumi

*A GIRL'S GOTTA DO, ETC.* was first produced by Theater Masters in Aspen, Colorado from February 4 – 7, 2017. The performance was directed by Daisy Walker, with sets by R. Thomas Ward and lighting by Cooper Mulderry and R. Thomas Ward. The production stage manager was Mark C. Hoffner. The cast was as follows:

**MALANA** .......................................... Emily Henley
**AVANA** ........................................... Ciara Morrison
**LEIGHANA** ....................................... Nakiri Gallagher

*A GIRL'S GOTTA DO, ETC.* was subsequently produced by Theater Masters and Theater for the New City in New York City from May 2 – 6, 2017. The performance was directed by Daisy Walker, with sets by R. Thomas Ward and lights by Chris Thielking. The production stage manager was Mark C. Hoffner. The cast was as follows:

**MALANA** ......................................... Andrea Morales
**AVANA** .......................................... Alexandra Lemus
**LEIGHANA** ........................................ Taylor Shurte

# CHARACTERS

**MALANA** – seventeen, a little too dramatic

**AVANA** – seventeen, a little too agreeable

**LEIGHANA** – seventeen, a little too out-there

*All three girls are simultaneously wise beyond their years and really, really not.

# SETTING

Malana's bedroom, which looks exactly like you'd imagine plus, like, one random heavy metal poster.

(**MALANA** *is wailing. Very loudly. Very, very loudly. Maybe she tries to speak words, but they are incomprehensible.* **AVANA** *and* **LEIGHANA** *sit on either side of her.* **AVANA** *listens and nods like she totally gets it.* **LEIGHANA** *is focused on* **MALANA** *but is also maybe thinking about what she's going to have for breakfast tomorrow.)*

*(When* **MALANA** *finally settles:)*

**AVANA.** Malana, I just cannot believe Jamie said that to you.

**LEIGHANA.** He's scum.

**AVANA.** I mean how could he disrespect you like that?

**LEIGHANA.** Disgusting.

**MALANA.** Dearest Ladies. Thank you so much for being here on this tragic day.

**LEIGHANA & AVANA.** You're welcome, Malana.

**AVANA.** I mean, you texted us a Code Susan, which we all know means to dispatch Lady Pact Number Forty-Two!

**ALL THREE.** Lady Pact Number Forty-Two:

**AVANA.** If either I, Avana –

**LEIGHANA.** Or I, Leighana –

**MALANA.** Or I, Malana –

**ALL THREE.** Call a Code Susan, the Ladies of Our Womanhood must assemble immediately.

**LEIGHANA.** I tried to get here so fast I only deodorized one armpit.

**MALANA.** Thank you for the sacrifice you made for me, Leighana.

**LEIGHANA.** You're welcome, Malana.

**MALANA.** If I die from a broken heart today, I am so glad to die in the company of the Ladies of Our Womanhood.

**AVANA**. Malana! You will survive this! You are a strong, smart, independent woman! And death by broken heart is statistically very rare!

**LEIGHANA**. And you're not allowed to die yet. Remember our Lady Pact Number Three?

**ALL THREE**. Lady Pact Number Three:

**LEIGHANA**. That I, Leighana –

**MALANA**. And I, Malana –

**AVANA**. And I, Avana –

**ALL THREE**. Shall topple the patriarchy by the age of forty.

**LEIGHANA**. At which point we will reconvene –

**MALANA**. Drink white wine –

**AVANA**. Eat overpriced salads –

**ALL THREE**. And reflect on our fulfilling lives together.

**AVANA**. Okay, so, Malana, in order to plan your next steps, we must review the details: You and Jamie were making out in the boys' locker room after third period chemistry –

**LEIGHANA**. The sexiest time.

**AVANA**. On top of a towel he lay down for you so you wouldn't get dusty –

**LEIGHANA**. The sexiest move.

**AVANA**. And then you took his sweaty face in your soft, delicate, cocoa-butter-moisturized hands –

**LEIGHANA**. The sexiest hands.

**MALANA**. Thank you, Leighana!

**LEIGHANA**. You're welcome, Malana!

**AVANA**. And you said –

**MALANA**. "Jamie Telofakis, will you do the honor of taking my virginity?"

**AVANA**. And he said –

**MALANA**. "No, that's okay."

> (**AVANA** and **LEIGHANA** gasp even though they've heard this story, like, twice.)

**AVANA**. How DARE he.

**LEIGHANA.** You gathered your courage, you put yourself out there, and he shut you down like a grocery store on a Sunday night.

**MALANA.** I just feel like I let you ladies down. I'm the only virgin left and I thought this was my chance to fulfill Lady Pact Number Thirty-Seven.

**ALL THREE.** Lady Pact Number Thirty-Seven:

**MALANA.** That I, Malana –

**LEIGHANA.** And I, Leighana –

**AVANA.** And I, Avana –

**ALL THREE.** Shall lose our virginities by senior year.

**AVANA.** You didn't let us down, Malana. You didn't do anything wrong!

**LEIGHANA.** Yeah, this is one hundred percent Jamie's fault. He denied your rights to your own womanhood. And by denying your rights, Malana, he denied us all.

**AVANA.** Ohmigod, Leighana, do you think Jamie was purposefully trying to sabotage Our Womanhood? Is this what a conspiracy theory is?

**LEIGHANA.** No, Avana. This is worse. This is…misogyny.

(**MALANA** *and* **AVANA** *gasp.*)

**MALANA.** How could I not see it before? I can't believe I almost lost my virginity to a misogynist!

**AVANA.** Malana. I am sorry to have to say this. But you have no choice but to…

| **AVANA.** | **LEIGHANA.** |
|---|---|
| Break up with him. | Kill him. |

**AVANA.** …Kill him?!

**LEIGHANA.** Sorry, is that not where we were at?

**MALANA.** Leighana, I don't know if that's a good idea. You know how blood makes me a little queasy.

**AVANA.** Blood?!

**LEIGHANA.** Oh, no, you wouldn't kill him directly. We'd ask the world to kill him for you.

MALANA. You mean like asking Oprah*?

LEIGHANA. So, confession: I have always had a bit of a sixth sense, and I've been practicing the spiritual arts a lot lately. And we can ask the spirits of the world to purposefully, accidentally kill Jamie in a non-violent way.

MALANA. Leighana, how have you never told us about your sixth sense?

LEIGHANA. I just recognize it's a privilege and I always want to check my privilege.

AVANA. Wait, wait, so we're really okay with...killing someone?

LEIGHANA. Jamie is a misogynist who disrespected our womanhood and violated Lady Pact Number Thirty-Seven. Aren't we all enraged by what he did?

MALANA. But my mother says rage is like a pimple. If you pop it, it could leave a scar on your face.

LEIGHANA. But Malana. Sometimes you pop a pimple. And you just look prettier.

MALANA. That is truly profound, Leighana.

LEIGHANA. I know.

AVANA. So...how exactly does this spiritual killing thing work?

LEIGHANA. Don't worry, Avana, it's pretty easy. I just need to create a center point. And then we need sacrifices. I need something new, something old, something pink and some booze.

MALANA. What about this tampon as something pink? The wrapper is pink. And it's unused. Can it also count as something new?

LEIGHANA. Yes, two-for-one! Spirits love bargains.

MALANA. And I have a CD for something old?

LEIGHANA. Great, spirits love vintage.

MALANA. I'm not sure if I can get alcohol, though. My father put a lock on his closet liquor stash.

---

*Or whoever the universally well-liked TV personality is at the time of production.

(**AVANA** *carefully goes into her bag and pulls out a flask.*)

**AVANA**. Um... We can use my secret flask?

**MALANA**. You have a flask? How classy of you!

**AVANA**. ...Thank you, Malana...

**MALANA**. You're welcome, Avana!

(**AVANA** *takes a quick swig when no one is looking. Meanwhile,* **LEIGHANA** *has made a beautiful structure out of, like, bed sheets and candy or something.*)

**LEIGHANA**. Okay, ladies, I have made the center.

**MALANA**. Leighana, did you just do that in the last thirty seconds?

**LEIGHANA**. Yeah I keep my talents hidden so no one expects too much from me. Now let us begin the peaceful death-invoking ceremony of the demonic darkness of the devil.

**AVANA**. Is Jamie really going to die?

**LEIGHANA**. It's all up to the spirits now. Okay Avana, you stand there, and I stand here, and, Malana, kneel in front – now Avana, hold my hands, and chant with me.

(*During the following,* **AVANA** *tries her best to say words at the same time as* **LEIGHANA**.)

Oh powers of the universe come to us now. Oh powers of Satan come to us now.

(*To* **MALANA**.) Okay, now start shimmying and doing violent movements and stuff.

(**MALANA** *does.*)

You look so cute. GREAT POWERS, SEE THIS INTELLIGENT BUT DEVASTATED WOMAN. SHE IS SHAKING! SHE DOES NOT DO THIS BECAUSE SHE IS A CRAZY PERSON. SHE DOES THIS BECAUSE A MAN HAS WRONGED HER. THAT MAN IS JAMIE TELOFAKIS. POWERS OF THE WORLD, FIND HIM! DO NOT GET DISTRACTED

BY HOW HOT HE IS. TEACH HIM NEVER TO DO
WRONG AGAIN. TAKE HIM DOWN AND –

> *(The lights flicker and* **LEIGHANA** *and* **AVANA**
> *scream.)*

**AVANA**. Ohmigod ohmigod ohmigod what did we do? Oh
no, oh no, what if we killed him?!

**MALANA**. Ladies, calm down, my mother probably plugged
in the toaster oven. It's very old and takes up a lot of
energy, just like my grandma at Thanksgiving dinner.

**AVANA**. Okay, okay, ladies, before we go any further, or, like,
do any death things, I have a confession: I know we
think Malana's the only virgin but...I actually am too.
I didn't sleep with Guber that one night in Pawtucket.
I just fell asleep on top of him while we watched the
movie *Lincoln.*\*

**MALANA**. Why did you lie to us?

**AVANA**. Because that was totally the perfect opportunity
and I didn't take it. I didn't want to disappoint you.

**MALANA**. Avana! We are your lady friends! We would not
have judged!

**LEIGHANA**. Of course not. *Lincoln* is so boring.

**MALANA**. And none of us *have* to have sex before senior
year.

**AVANA**. But what about Lady Pact Number Thirty-Seven?

**MALANA**. Those pacts provide us with fun goals. But they
shouldn't pressure any of us to do anything we're not
ready for.

**LEIGHANA**. Yeah, I'm sorry if trying to spiritually kill Jamie
made you feel bad about keeping your v-card.

**AVANA**. You ladies are all of my womanhood! Thank you
for understanding.

**MALANA & LEIGHANA**. You're welcome, Avana!

**AVANA**. I cannot wait until we're forty.

**MALANA**. And drinking wine?

---

\*Or another film that is widely renowned but long and wordy.

**LEIGHANA.** And eating salads?

**AVANA.** And reflecting on how we smashed the patriarchy together!

**MALANA.** Who needs Jamie? Or any men? If I have the Ladies of Our Womanhood.

**LEIGHANA.** Yeah, who needs heels or makeup just to impress them?

**MALANA.** Who needs to accommodate their emotional unavailabilities?

**LEIGHANA.** And who needs penises anyway?

**AVANA.** And who needs to shave!

| **LEIGHANA.** | **MALANA.** |
|---|---|
| Oh I definitely do. | I just feel like it's more hygienic. |

**AVANA.** Oh?

**MALANA.** Let's make a new Lady Pact. That I, Malana.

**LEIGHANA.** And I, Leighana –

**AVANA.** And I, Avana –

**MALANA.** Will make a conscious effort –

**LEIGHANA & AVANA.** Will make a conscious effort.

**MALANA.** Not to let human males –

**LEIGHANA & AVANA.** Not to let human males.

**MALANA.** Majorly influence our emotional well-beings!

**LEIGHANA & AVANA.** Majorly influence our emotional well-beings –

**AVANA.** Because we have agency!

**LEIGHANA.** Avana, I think that makes the sentence too long.

**AVANA.** Ohmigod I'm so sorry.

**LEIGHANA.** What number Lady Pact is this?

**AVANA.** I think it's number two hundred and sixty –

(**MALANA** *gets a text and screams.*)

**MALANA.** OMG Jamie just texted me. He said he was feeling gassy earlier, but wanted to remind me that I am "hotter and also smarter than most of the school..."

*(Pause for a moment as they consider this. Then all three **LADIES** squeal.)*

**MALANA.** Shh! He's typing! ...He wants to meet me in the Burger King bathroom right now!

**AVANA.** Ohmigod, ohmigod!

**LEIGHANA.** Jamie respects you so much.

**AVANA.** You are SO lucky, Malana.

**LEIGHANA.** We have to make you look hot ASAP.

**AVANA.** You're gonna have the best time.

**MALANA.** I am so glad you ladies are here for this amazing moment. It is so easy to be a woman in this world when I have friends like you.

*(They start laughing. It starts as little girlish giggles, but then they progress to hysterical laughter. We hear thunder and the lights flicker.)*

*(The three **GIRLS** become three **WOMEN** holding salads and glasses of wine. They are still laughing.)*

*(Then they end their laughter by taking a collective sigh together.)*

*(There is a brief pause where they all look exhausted.)*

*(Lights out.)*

**End of Play**

# A Last Night on Earth

Hannah Doran

*A LAST NIGHT ON EARTH* was first produced by Theater Masters in Aspen, Colorado from February 4 – 7, 2017. The performance was directed by Lee Kasper, with sets by R. Thomas Ward and lighting by Cooper Mulderry and R. Thomas Ward. The production stage manager was Mark C. Hoffner. The cast was as follows:

**SHURA** . . . . . . . . . . . . . . . . . . . . . . . . . . . . . . . . . . . . . . . . . . . . . . . . . . Brittany Bays

**MRS. DAY** . . . . . . . . . . . . . . . . . . . . . . . . . . . . . . . . . . . . . . . . . . . . .Linda Carnes

*A LAST NIGHT ON EARTH* was subsequently produced by Theater Masters and Theater for the New City in New York City from May 2 – 6, 2017. The performance was directed by Lee Kasper, with sets by R. Thomas Ward and lights by Chris Thielking. The production stage manager was Mark C. Hoffner. The cast was as follows:

**SHURA** . . . . . . . . . . . . . . . . . . . . . . . . . . . . . . . . . . . . . . . . . . . . Rebekah Brockman

**MRS. DAY** . . . . . . . . . . . . . . . . . . . . . . . . . . . . . . . . . . . . . . . . . . . . . . Joan Porter

# CHARACTERS

**SHURA** – Thirty-six. Former juvenile inmate. Has been on death row since she was old enough. Killed a classmate. Strong-looking. White scars line her wrists from prior suicide attempts.

**MRS. DAY** – Late sixties. Mother of the girl Shura killed. Slim, but has not aged well. Dressed quite conservatively; she makes an effort, if only for herself.

# SETTING

The action takes place in the visitation cell of a U.S. penitentiary.

# TIME

January 2005

# AUTHOR'S NOTES

The writer imagines Mrs. Day as an African American woman. This idea need not be adhered to. However, if Shura is played by a black actor, Mrs. Day must not be white. Any other racial casting combination is acceptable.

The actor should resist the urge to play Shura as hysterical. She is emotional but we should not regard her as "crazy."

Much of this play – perhaps one-third – is silence. They don't know what to say or how to say it. Their conversation is heavy with awkward pauses.

*(Lights up.)*

*(A chair sits before a glass window in the center of the room; on the other side of the glass, a matching chair. Two large analog clocks on the back wall, one on each side, read 10:41 p.m.)*

*(**SHURA** lies on her back on the floor. Her execution will be taking place in under three hours. On the chair is a bucket of stone-cold fried chicken.)*

*(**MRS. DAY** stands, awkwardly and clutching her purse, behind the chair on the visitors' side. She has just entered; **SHURA** hasn't seen her yet.)*

*(When they speak, their conversation is, at first, very stilted. **MRS. DAY** steps forward.)*

MRS. DAY. Hello, Shura.

*(**SHURA** sits up quickly and stares at **MRS. DAY** through the glass in profound surprise. She has not seen her in twenty-two years but knows exactly who she is.)*

Can you hear me?

SHURA. *(Nods, before vocalising.)* Yes. They told me I had a visitor.

MRS. DAY. Well. Here I am.

SHURA. Here you are.

MRS. DAY. I'm a little late. Did they tell you I'd be late?

SHURA. I... I thought –

MRS. DAY. Yes?

SHURA. Nothing.

*(Pause.)*

**SHURA.** I thought it – would be my mom.

**MRS. DAY.** There's quite a crowd out there, you know. You're all over the local news.

**SHURA.** This is big. I'm the first woman in thirteen years.

(*An uncomfortable silence.* **MRS. DAY** *glances up at the clock.*)

**MRS. DAY.** You don't have much time. Not that I need to tell you. But I can't stay long.

**SHURA.** (*Getting up. She has had this meeting prepared forever, and now she's forgotten everything she wants to say.*) Okay... I didn't expect you. I just... I – I want you to know that I'm not bitter. That this is happening.

**MRS. DAY.** I'm so glad you've found some inner peace.

**SHURA.** Please. Sit down.

(**MRS. DAY** *hesitates, then walks over and sits.*)

I want to tell you...I guess...why I did it. Why I killed your daughter.

**MRS. DAY.** (*Slight hesitation.*) You always said you didn't know why.

**SHURA.** Well – I don't. But –

**MRS. DAY.** You want closure. That's what this is about.

(**SHURA** *nods.*)

Well great. Isn't that admirable.

**SHURA.** So do you.

**MRS. DAY.** Excuse me?

**SHURA.** Why else would you be here?

**MRS. DAY.** I – thought I should come.

**SHURA.** Yeah. First time in twenty-two years. I requested visits, I tried to contact you –

**MRS. DAY.** How *dare* you. I have no obligation to see you. You can't make me feel guilty –

**SHURA.** I'm not –

**MRS. DAY.** You want to tie up all the loose ends before you die, and I'm a loose end, aren't I?

*(No response.)*

You think you can fix everything now, and it'll be a straight path right up to heaven.

**SHURA.** I – I'm not what you think. I'm not a monster.

**MRS. DAY.** No?

**SHURA.** I regret what I did.

> *(**MRS. DAY** nods. She expected this.)*

**MRS. DAY.** Funny. Don't you think it's a little late for that?

**SHURA.** I am…uh. Remorseful.

**MRS. DAY.** I don't want to hear it.

**SHURA.** I have remorse for my actions.

**MRS. DAY.** No you don't.

**SHURA.** I do!

**MRS. DAY.** Don't lie to me.

**SHURA.** I'm not –

**MRS. DAY.** False contrition won't save you now.

**SHURA.** It's not false –

**MRS. DAY.** I don't believe you know the meaning of remorse.

> *(Maddened, **SHURA** kicks the bucket of chicken off the chair. **MRS. DAY** jumps, but is safe on the other side of the glass. **SHURA** leans forward on the table so her nose is almost touching the window.)*

**SHURA.** *(Growling.)* Yes I do.

> *(A clanging noise from outside the room as someone bashes on the door. **SHURA** stands straight, sighs, and picks up the chicken from the floor. **MRS. DAY** watches. Pause.)*

**MRS. DAY.** Fried chicken… You haven't eaten it.

**SHURA.** I drank the coffee.

**MRS. DAY.** I wouldn't have thought caffeine would be necessary.

> *(Pause. She regrets this comment.)*
>
> *(**SHURA** looks at her.)*

**SHURA.** I don't eat meat.

> (**MRS. DAY** *stares.* **SHURA** *stares back defensively.*)

Everyone asks for fried stuff.

**MRS. DAY.** Comfort food. From your childhood.

> (**SHURA** *looks at her, puzzled.*)

You used to eat fried chicken together. You and – and Claire.

*(Quietly, remembering.)* Grease all round your mouths.

**SHURA.** My mom would give it to us.

> *(Pause.)*

**MRS. DAY.** I see her sometimes. At the store. The hair salon.

> (**SHURA** *sets down the bucket and sighs. Beat.*)

**SHURA.** That day. I... I was –

**MRS. DAY.** I'm not here to share your last supper and break bread and tell you it's all okay.

**SHURA.** Then why *are* you here?

> (**MRS. DAY** *struggles to respond.*)

Are you going to watch?

**MRS. DAY.** *(She takes this in, incredulous.)* Watch?

**SHURA.** *(Hastily.)* I just...wondered.

> (**MRS. DAY** *shakes her head. Beat.*)

I was tired. That day. I was just...tired.

**MRS. DAY.** Tired?

**SHURA.** She beat me at cards.

> (**MRS. DAY,** *very still, stares at* **SHURA.**)

There was a bee...

**MRS. DAY.** A bee.

**SHURA.** A bee, a bumblebee, flying around the room, driving itself insane, driving *me*... Buzzing round and round. All the windows were closed. It was trapped. It was a stifling hot day. I was sweating, I couldn't focus. And she was winning.

**MRS. DAY**. *(Raising her hands. A barely-voiced whisper.)* Please...

**SHURA**. *(Talking more and more rapidly.)* She *always* won. She was so good. She won everything, Mrs. Day, you know that, she was...so smart and, and –

**MRS. DAY**. Please stop.

**SHURA**. And I had this pen-knife in my pocket; I had taken it from –

> *(***MRS. DAY*** stands.)*

Wait! Let me tell you –

**MRS. DAY**. You've told me enough.

> *(She turns to go.)*

**SHURA**. *(Stands, hands against the glass, trying to make her listen as she walks away.)* Please! I didn't know, until I had done it, and the blood came in thick patches on her dress – and I was sorry then and I'm sorry now! Please. I have to tell you.

**MRS. DAY**. You're *hurting me.*

**SHURA**. I dream of her every night – I dream of her dancing; she wanted to be a dancer, didn't she?

**MRS. DAY**. Stop it!

**SHURA**. It was over so quickly –

**MRS. DAY**. No, it wasn't.

**SHURA**. I know what I did –

**MRS. DAY**. No, you don't! There are details they...*spared* you from in court. Claire didn't die immediately –

**SHURA**. I know.

**MRS. DAY**. – After you'd run away, she crawled to the phone and called my office. My boss answered. And Claire just said...she said...

**SHURA**. "Tell my mom I'm dying."

> *(***MRS. DAY*** stares at her.)*

I was... I...

**MRS. DAY**. You were still there.

(**SHURA** *moans gently.*)

**MRS. DAY.** My God...

**SHURA.** *(Leaning against the glass; a despairing croak building to a wail.)* I'm *sorry.* I'm so sorry. Please. I'm sorry, I'm sorry, I'm s*orry.*

> *(A long, long silence. There is nothing left to say.* **MRS. DAY** *stands very still, and then turns to leave.)*

Mrs. Day...? Mrs. Day! Wait!

> *(***MRS. DAY*** *exits. The door clatters behind her.)*

Mrs. Day!

> *(***SHURA*** *leans her head against the glass. A silence. She turns and looks at the chicken. Beat.)*
>
> *(Blackout.)*

**End of Play**

# A Short Man
# and the Eyeballs

Yi Hsuan Tseng

*A SHORT MAN AND THE EYEBALLS* was first produced by Theater Masters in Aspen, Colorado from February 4 – 7, 2017. The performance was directed by Stephen Cedars, with sets by R. Thomas Ward and lighting by Cooper Mulderry and R. Thomas Ward. The production stage manager was Mark C. Hoffner. The cast was as follows:

**EYEBALL A**..................................... Morgan Walsh
**EYEBALL B**.......................................Daniel Barnes
**EYEBALL C**..................................... Shelly Marolt
**EYEBALL D**......................................Heather Ardley
**SHORT MAN** ..................................... Willie Moseley

*A SHORT MAN AND THE EYEBALLS* was subsequently produced by Theater Masters and Theater for the New City in New York City from May 2 – 6, 2017. The performance was directed by Stephen Cedars, with sets by R. Thomas Ward and lights by Chris Thielking. The production stage manager was Mark C. Hoffner. The cast was as follows:

**EYEBALL A**...................................Rebekah Brockman
**EYEBALL B**..................................... Andrea Morales
**EYEBALL C**..................................... Rebecca White
**EYEBALL D**....................................... Will Manning
**SHORT MAN** ..................................... Pietro Gonzalez

# CHARACTERS

EYEBALL A
EYEBALL B
EYEBALL C
EYEBALL D
SHORT MAN

*(Lights up.)*

*(A huge image of a woman's face upstage. The only thing that has to be distinguished is a pair of* **EYEBALLS**. *The stage is filled with many mannequins without their heads. They are set in paired dancing positions.)*

*(A* **SHORT MAN** *sets up a video camera and starts recording. There are two actors standing on either side behind the* **SHORT MAN**. *They represent the two* **EYEBALLS** *of the* **SHORT MAN**. *The* **SHORT MAN** *yawns, he puts eye drops on his eyes. The two* **EYEBALLS** *react to it.)*

**EYEBALL A**. When you see this video, I may finally close up.

**EYEBALL B**. But I need to tell you now before WE forget it all, you were somebody once.

**EYEBALL A**. You meant something.

**EYEBALL B**. You were not nobody.

**SHORT MAN**. It's been nine years, two hundred and fourteen days, eleven hours and fifty-five minutes since the last time YOU got sleep. It's because the minute before this nine years, two hundred and fourteen days, eleven hours and fifty-five minutes, YOU met a pair of eyeballs.

*(Beat.)*

I think I'd better introduce myself a little. Hi, I'm a short man and that's how the people see me and call me. Sometimes, people crash into me by accident, even if they never see me, they still apologize, so please, don't misunderstand. I'm not a tragic figure in any fairy tale, this is just the way how I was born.

*(Beat.)*

**SHORT MAN**. My mom told me when God closes a door, somewhere he opens a window. In school, he might have closed the door on basketball, but he opened a math class for me. I'm not saying I'm good at math, but I'm really good at memorizing.

> *(Beat.)*

Pi is equal to 3.141592653589793238462643383279502884197169399375105820974... I can tell you all the numbers that I memorized, but I don't think that's a good idea. When I was in school, I learned I only needed to answer 3.14. Whenever I answered five more numbers, my classmates got freaked out. Another five numbers, they started making fun of me. Also the teacher stopped me, but not the laughing.

> *(Beat.)*

I have this ability of memorizing. As my mom said, this is the window that God gave me. Even though it didn't help much in my childhood, but this window helps me to portray the moment when WE met that pair of eyeballs precisely.

> *(The **SHORT MAN** lights up a cigarette. He takes a deep breath and blows out the smoke.)*

I walk into a bar. As usual, no one sees me, even the security guard. A romantic love song is playing, all the people are pairing up automatically. They hold each other, they dance with each other, they move as one person. They swing, swing, and swing, and I'm just ignored and short.

I scan the bar. Many colors of neon lights sparkle around the couples, like bubbles. They are light, smooth, and tender. My sight travels through the bubbles, everyone is twisted inside. Boom! Bang! Bomb! A finger. A huge finger from a woman. It breaks all the bubbles. The only thing left is a pair of eyes. A pair of eyeballs. Now, I see!

> *(The **SHORT MAN** closes his eyes. The two **EYEBALLS** sing a love song.)*

HEY! YOU THERE!
PLEASE, LOOK HERE.
WE ARE A PAIR OF EYEBALLS.
AND SO ARE YOU.
YOU SEE WHAT I SEE,
I SEE WHAT YOU SEE.
OH! THAT'S ME.

HEY! YOU THERE!
PLEASE, LOOK HERE.
WE ARE A PAIR OF EYEBALLS.
AND SO ARE YOU.
I WANT TO GIVE YOU A ROSE,
SO I HOLD THE MUD,
WOULD YOU LIKE TO PUT A LOVE SEED INTO MY HANDS?

**EYEBALL A.** Hey, do you see those sexy twins?

**EYEBALL B.** Yes.

**EYEBALL A.** Do you think they are watching us?

**EYEBALL B.** No.

**EYEBALL A.** Why?

**EYEBALL B.** Because we are short, and no one sees us.

**EYEBALL A.** We should get them to see us! It never hurts.

**EYEBALL B.** No, it hurt last time. Do you remember the last
time...

**EYEBALL A.** No, I don't. Are you with me?

**EYEBALL B.** What do you mean?

**EYEBALL A.** I mean are you with me?

**EYEBALL B.** Sure, we are a pair of eyeballs.

**EYEBALL A.** Then do this with me.

> *(They both take a deep bow to the front. After,
> they stand up straight like two warriors.
> They try to hold their positions as long as
> they can.)*

> *(After, they take a bow to the front.)*

See! They are watching us.

**EYEBALL B.** This is exactly what you told me last time. Do
you remember the last time when we tried to get some

eyeballs to see us, but there were two other eyeballs coming toward us, they were huge as two basketballs, and we hate basketballs...

**EYEBALL A.** Then we ran away.

**EYEBALL B.** Okay, great. Now you remember.

**EYEBALL A.** Yes, even I remember everything, so what?

**EYEBALL B.** So you should also remember what did they say to us...

**EYEBALL A.** They said, "Hey short boys! What are you guys looking at?"

**EYEBALL B.** They said, "Are you guys looking for trouble?"

*(Another pair of* **EYEBALLS**, **C** *and* **D**, *from another man appear onstage.)*

**EYEBALL C.** Hey short boys! What are you guys looking at?

**EYEBALL D.** Are you guys looking for trouble?

*(***EYEBALLS C** *and* **D** *laugh.)*

**EYEBALL B.** God, this is happening again...

**EYEBALL A.** Hey! Are you guys staring at us?

**EYEBALL C.** You don't need to worry, we are definitely not watching you dwarves.

**EYEBALL D.** Yeah, we are watching those sexy twins.

**EYEBALL A.** So are we.

**EYEBALL B.** But we don't want to get in trouble.

**EYEBALL C.** Too late.

**EYEBALL D.** Because you already are.

*(***EYEBALLS A**, **B**, **C**, *and* **D** *stand as tall as they can. After, they take a bow to the front.)*

**EYEBALL A.** We need to be tough this time, this is our chance, we want to be seen.

**EYEBALL B.** But not by those basketballs.

**EYEBALL C.** Hey short boys! Here's a trouble.

**EYEBALL D.** Are those twins staring at you guys or us?

**EYEBALL B.** Hmm...we're not sure.

**EYEBALL A.** No, we're sure. It's us.

**EYEBALL C.** What makes you so sure?

**EYEBALL B.** Yes, what makes you so sure?

**EYEBALL A.** Because I can just tell by the way how they're staring at this direction. They're staring at us!

**EYEBALL B, C & D.** What the fuck?

**EYEBALL D.** That doesn't make sense.

**EYEBALL A.** Why?

**EYEBALL C.** Because I can ALSO tell by the way how they're staring at this direction. They're DEFINITELY staring at us.

**EYEBALL A.** That's bullshit! You just copy what I said!

**EYEBALL B.** I think we all need to chill.

**EYEBALL D.** Your partner doesn't look like he wants to chill.

**EYEBALL C.** Maybe he wants some fights!

**EYEBALL B.** Wait! Why can't we just go ask the twins who they are staring at? And the problem will be solved.

**EYEBALL D.** That's not necessary.

**EYEBALL A.** We can keep it simple.

**EYEBALL C.** If you want to know who they're staring at.

**EYEBALL A, C & D.** That would be easier, if only two of us are sitting at this direction.

> (*The two groups of* **EYEBALLS** *bow rapidly. They both make the noise of punching, shouting, and fighting. At the end,* **EYEBALL B** *bends its body.* **EYEBALL A** *can barely stand straight.*)

**EYEBALL A.** Are you all right?

**EYEBALL B.** No, I'm not. I'm swollen, and we got beaten.

> (*The* **SHORT MAN** *opens his one eye only.*)

**SHORT MAN.** I got beat up. I'm lying on the floor, and one of my hands holds my swollen eye. I'm not trying to cover the bruising. I just don't want anyone to find out I'm crying. God! I'm crying, crying with only one of my eyes. But yes! Now everyone sees me. The first time that all the eyeballs are watching me...watching the moment that...

**EYEBALL A.** Do you see that?

**EYEBALL B.** I can't see, I'm swollen.

**EYEBALL A.** We made it.

**EYEBALL B.** What?

**SHORT MAN.** ...She's walking up to me.

**EYEBALL B.** Who?

**EYEBALL A.** Those twins.

**SHORT MAN.** That pair of eyes.

**EYEBALL B.** Damn it. I can't see. I can't see. What should we do now?

**SHORT MAN.** I don't know...

**EYEBALL A.** Should we say hi?

**EYEBALL B.** Should we ask her name?

**EYEBALL A.** Should we ask her phone number?

**EYEBALL B.** Should we give her a blink?

**SHORT MAN.** I don't know...

**EYEBALL A.** Just say something!

> (**EYEBALL A** *stands straight, but* **EYEBALL B** *still bends its body.*)

**SHORT MAN.** So...were you staring at me or not?

**EYEBALL A & B.** What the fuck!!

> (*Suddenly,* **EYEBALL A** *bows too.*)

And I passed out.

> (**EYEBALLS C** *and* **D** *exit.*)

The moment when I regained consciousness. The doctor told me, my eye will be fine, but my brain got permanent damage from the fight, and that will affect my ability of memorizing. I'll gradually lose all of my memories. I can still see what I see, but I won't remember what I see, then everything means nothing to me. After, every time I woke up, some of my memories were gone...

(**EYEBALLS A** *and* **B** *stand up. They are exhausted.*)

**EYEBALL A.** Hey! Are you still there?

**EYEBALL B.** Yes... Yes... Yes...

**EYEBALL A.** I thought you were sleeping.

**EYEBALL B.** That was close.

**EYEBALL A.** We can't sleep. Stay with me.

**EYEBALL B.** Why? I'm so tired.

**EYEBALL A.** Because every time we slept, some of our memories disappeared.

**EYEBALL B.** So what?

**EYEBALL A.** So we will forget who we are.

**EYEBALL B.** It doesn't matter. We were nobody.

**EYEBALL A.** No. We have been seen once in the bar. We were somebody, and we can't forget it.

**EYEBALL B.** Yes, we meant something.

**EYEBALL A.** We need to fight.

**SHORT MAN.** So I decided, I will never sleep anymore, and that's the way I protect my memories, and that's the way I protect who I am... I am somebody...

> (*The* **SHORT MAN** *lights up a cigarette, takes a deep breath, and blows out the smoke.*)

But no one can fight against time, at least I tried, YOU tried, and WE tried. Everything becomes a blur. Our memories are like smoke. You can see it, you can blow it, you can wave your hands at it, but you can't ever catch it. When the smoke is gone, nothing is left. When YOU see this video, I may finally close up my eyes which means WE eventually lost everything. I'm recording this video, it's not for anyone else, it's for you, for myself – the short man. I need to tell you before WE forget it all, you were somebody once, you meant something, you weren't nobody, even if it only happened once. Now, go get a nice sleep that you deserve. I know, you'll be fine just like Mom told us, when God closes a door, somewhere he opens a window, there always is another window waiting for us...

> *(The **SHORT MAN** blows up the smoke covering the entire huge image of the woman's face. He closes up his eyes. **EYEBALLS A** and **B** take a bow and hold. Suddenly, the huge image of the woman's face becomes a window.)*
>
> *(It opens. Fade out.)*

### End of Play

# Everything You'll Miss in Minutes

Lauren Wimmer

*EVERYTHING YOU'LL MISS IN MINUTES* was first produced by Theater Masters in Aspen, Colorado from February 4 – 7, 2017. The performance was directed by Lee Kasper, with sets by R. Thomas Ward and lighting by Cooper Mulderry and R. Thomas Ward. The production stage manager was Mark C. Hoffner. The cast was as follows:

**SYDNEY** . . . . . . . . . . . . . . . . . . . . . . . . . . . . . . . . . . . . . . . . . . . . . . . Izzi Rojo
**HC** . . . . . . . . . . . . . . . . . . . . . . . . . . . . . . . . . . . . . . . . . . . . Talullah Marolt
**PERRY** . . . . . . . . . . . . . . . . . . . . . . . . . . . . . . . . . . . . . . . . . Franz Alderfer

*EVERYTHING YOU'LL MISS IN MINUTES* was subsequently produced by Theater Masters and Theater for the New City in New York City from May 2 – 6, 2017. The performance was directed by Lee Kasper, with sets by R. Thomas Ward and lights by Chris Thielking. The production stage manager was Mark C. Hoffner. The cast was as follows:

**SYDNEY** . . . . . . . . . . . . . . . . . . . . . . . . . . . . . . . . . . . . . . . . Alexandra Lemus
**HC** . . . . . . . . . . . . . . . . . . . . . . . . . . . . . . . . . . . . . . . . . . Andrea Morales
**PERRY** . . . . . . . . . . . . . . . . . . . . . . . . . . . . . . . . . . . . . . . . Matthew Lawler

## CHARACTERS

**SYDNEY** – female, fifteen years old
**HC** – female, fourteen years old
**PERRY** – male, forty-five years old

## SETTING

Big Burn Mountain chairlift

## TIME

Midday

## AUTHOR'S NOTES

A slash ( / ) signifies an interruption in dialogue by the following line.

Perry's lines are said in the exact same cheery way each time.

Although it states that the actors are wearing snowboards and skis, the actors should not wear actual skis and snowboards.

*(**SYDNEY** and **HC** sit on a stalled, rickety chairlift. **PERRY** sits between them. **SYDNEY** and **HC** wear snowboards while **PERRY** wears skis. They're all dressed in winter outerwear.)*

| HC. | SYDNEY. |
|---|---|
| Are you sure that Dad's ashes are fine sitting between us? Shouldn't one of us hold them? Him? I dunno what to say. It's "him," right? Or should I say "it"? | He's fine. Don't worry about it. You'll never get anywhere worrying about it. Relax. Uh-huh. Yeah. I know. |

**PERRY**. Meet me at the Big Burn chairlift at two o'clock.

**HC**. Sydney, you're not listening to me! We've been sitting on this stalled chairlift for.ev.er!

**SYDNEY**. Uh-huh. Yeah. What?

**HC**. Dad's ashes will fall if he, they, it, sits between us like this.

**SYDNEY**. Whatever.

**HC**. Hold it?

**SYDNEY**. Ewwww. No. What happens if he spills on me? If it spills on me. They spill on me. Just leave it.

**PERRY**. Meet me at the Big Burn chairlift at two o'clock.

**HC**. This is so morbid.

**SYDNEY**. It's what he wanted.

**HC**. I don't think he knew he would die / this way.

**SYDNEY**. Uh-huh. Yeah. I know.

**HC**. That he would fall off a chairlift. This chairlift. It's what it said in the will though. That he wanted to be scattered on top of the Big Burn. When should we scatter him?

**SYDNEY**. On top of the mountain. Over the precipice. Like he wanted.

| **HC**. | **SYDNEY**. |
|---|---|
| We've been sitting here forever. Oh my God. Can you hold him? Can you hold him. | I can't right now. I can't. I just can't. I can't even right now. I just can't even a little bit. |

**PERRY**. Meet me at the Big Burn chairlift at two o'clock.

**SYDNEY**. I can't cry. I can't cry. I can't cry.

**HC**. You're crying.

**SYDNEY**. Shut up! I'm a female snowboarder. I don't shed tears, I shred slopes. I can't cry. I can't cry. I can't cry, but I think about all the firsts, lasts, happies, sads, couldas, wouldas, shouldas, embarrassings he will miss out on.

> *(A big whiff of snow following a gust of wind strikes the chairlift.)*

**HC**. Like my first pot brownie I will experience in six months and two days from now.

**SYDNEY**. More like your last pot brownie.

**HC**. I will find the brownies underneath Dad's bed in a shoe box. And I'll wonder, "If he's been hiding baked goods from me, what else could he be hiding?" I'll wonder if Dad was high the day he died. I'll wonder if Dad wished he could smoke pot with me, but knew I was too young.

**SYDNEY**. Not something you'd want to do with your daughter.

**HC**. Dad was different.

> *(A big whiff of snow following a gust of wind strikes the chairlift.)*

I think I'm dying! I just ate brownies and I don't feel like me, I don't feel like I'm in my skin, is someone else in my skin? Dad, I think I'm dying.

**SYDNEY**. I think what she's trying to tell you is that there was pot in them. Dad, aren't you gonna yell at her?

**PERRY**. Meet me at the Big Burn chairlift at two o'clock.

*(A big whiff of snow following a gust of wind strikes the chairlift.)*

**SYDNEY**. Or getting my driver's license which I will experience in one year, four months, and twenty-three days from now. I'll drive Dad's old car. It has his smell. Cigarettes and aftershave. I only listen to the Classic Rock station 'cause that's what he listened to. And driving on the freeway, I'll feel free for the first time.

**HC**. A little reckless.

**SYDNEY**. But I'll be so happy. Maybe too free. I'll wish I had someone to yell at me for it.

**HC**. SYDNEY, YOU NEED TO DRIVE MORE CAREFULLY –

**SYDNEY**. I meant, like, someone older.

**HC**. Whoops.

*(A big whiff of snow following a gust of wind strikes the chairlift.)*

**SYDNEY**. I can drive myself to soccer now, Dad! I don't need you.

**HC**. She also just wants to make out with her boyfriend at Burrows Creek.

**SYDNEY**. Shut up!

**PERRY**. Meet me at the Big Burn chairlift at two o'clock.

*(A big whiff of snow following a gust of wind strikes the chairlift.)*

**SYDNEY**. In two years, four months, and five days from today, I'll lose my virginity right in the backseat of Dad's indigo Volvo I've named Tom.

**HC**. I'll cringe when you tell me. Putting my hands over my ears going, "Lalalalalalalalalalalala."

**SYDNEY.** I'll love retelling each sweaty, slippery, sinful detail. Like how he –

**HC.** Lalalalalalalalalalala I'll have my first alcoholic beverage in seven years, three months, and seven days from now.

**SYDNEY.** Gross. No one calls it that.

**HC.** My first booze.

**SYDNEY.** Although it won't be your first. It'll be your, what number will it be?

**HC.** I won't be able to count that high on two hands. I have a flask in my jacket pocket right now full of Mike's Hard. I'll down it in fifty-three minutes from now in the Big Burn Pizza Place bathroom.

**SYDNEY.** I'll see the flask peek out of your jacket pocket and I'll want to get mad at you just like Dad would've done, but I'll, I'll, I'll –

> (*A big whiff of snow following a gust of wind strikes the chairlift.*)

HC's first beer!

**HC.** Yeah. Totally my first beer.

**SYDNEY.** And she totally won't get drunk after this night. Right, Dad?

**PERRY.** Meet me at the Big Burn chairlift at two o'clock.

> (*A big whiff of snow following a gust of wind strikes the chairlift.*)

**SYDNEY.** I'll never get married. Twenty years and fifteen days from today I still won't be married. I mean, it didn't work out for Mom and Dad so what's the point?

**HC.** I will get married and it will be so beautiful and the woman will be so beautiful and it'll be everything I could ever want. Everything I could ever need. Eleven years and two months and three days from today I will be married! It maybe didn't work out for Mom and Dad, but I'm different!

**SYDNEY.** Good for you.

> (*A big whiff of snow following a gust of wind strikes the chairlift.*)

**SYDNEY.**

I'm never getting married. It's a social construct and I can love without a ring, or a ceremony, or a cake, or a wedding day that my whole family will sit through knowing I will be sleeping with my husband that night. It's just grotesque. I mean, who needs that? Who?

**HC.**

That's so sad. Awwww. That's really unfortunate, Sydney. That really is. Tell me more. Tell me how you really feel, Sydney. I'm just keeping my options open for the right woman. Looking. Looking. Looking. Looking. Found her. Never mind. Never liked her that much anyway. Looking. Looking. Looking. Found her. Keeping her. Will you walk me down the aisle, Dad?

**PERRY.** Meet me at the Big Burn chairlift at two o'clock.

*(A big whiff of snow following a gust of wind strikes the chairlift.)*

**SYDNEY.** In nineteen years and eleven months and three days from now I'll faint at work, but I'll pass it off as a joke. I'll laugh, but I'll run to the bathroom and cry. I'll dial Dad's number all these years later. It'll go through, but it will be a teenage kid working at Don Marino's Pizza asking if I want a slice.

**HC.** I'll be too busy. In nineteen years and ten months and twenty-two days from today I'll have a baby, Lily, adopted from Arkansas. I'll feel every emotion, but I'll glide through as seamlessly as my snowboard gliding around moguls.

**SYDNEY.** When I meet Lily for the first and only time, I'll see a lot of myself in her.

*(A big whiff of snow following a gust of wind strikes the chairlift.)*

My hair keeps coming out in chunks. And I don't know why. I used to be a female snowboarder. Now I'm just a female crier. / My throat. It bleeds. And bleeds. And bleeds.

**HC**. Her name's "Lily." From Arkansas. Dad, you wanna hold her? She's a little squirrely.

**PERRY**. Meet me at the Big Burn chairlift at two o'clock.

**HC**. She likes you. She loves her granddaddy, doesn't she? Don't you, Lily?

**SYDNEY**. I'm all knots and tears and fears and weakness and a big cloud of thoughts like the ones you see in cartoons. Dad, don't cry. I will try to outlive you in my own selfish way.

**HC**. I'll hold your hand as you take your final breath, Sydney.

**PERRY**. Meet me at the Big Burn chairlift at two o'clock.

> *(A big whiff of snow following a gust of wind strikes the chairlift.)*

**SYDNEY**. I'll die in twenty years and fifteen days from today.

> *(Silence.)*

**HC**. I will wish I was there more. But I won't be far behind, Sydney. Don't worry.

**PERRY**. Meet –

**SYDNEY**. How?

**PERRY**. Me –

**HC**. What?

**PERRY**. At –

**SYDNEY**. How will you die?

**PERRY**. TheBigBurnchairliftattwoo'clock.

> *(A huge, catastrophic heap of snow following a gust of wind strikes the chairlift to the point where the audience can no longer see **SYDNEY**, **HC**, or **PERRY**. Another gust of wind strikes the chairlift so the audience can now see **SYDNEY** and **HC**. **PERRY** is no longer present.)*

| HC. | SYDNEY. |
|---|---|
| He fell! I told you to look after him! I told you to hold him! I told you. I told you. You never listen to me! If you're not gonna listen to me, then I'll, I'll, I'll, I'll make you. | I'm sorry! I should have held him! I should have! I'm sorry. I didn't know, I don't know what I'm doing. |

*(HC's tears turn into laughter.)*

**HC.** Just the way he died.

**SYDNEY.** You're right. Through a chairlift. I didn't mean to, HC.

**HC.** Just like Dad didn't mean to –

**SYDNEY.** Although sometimes I wonder if he meant to, but that's just a thought.

**HC.** I thought that too.

**SYDNEY.** You think?

**HC.** Sometimes. Yeah. You?

**SYDNEY.** I do. I really do. But why?

**HC.** Don't ask.

**SYDNEY.** Why?

**HC.** Don't think about it. I do too much thinking.

**SYDNEY.** I do too much "Uh-huh. Yeah. Really. Yeah."

**HC.** Just like Dad.

**SYDNEY.** I'm not him.

**HC.** I'm not him.

**SYDNEY.** I'm me.

**HC.** Sometimes I wanna be you.

**SYDNEY.** Sometimes I wanna be you too.

**HC.** Sometimes I wanna be him.

**SYDNEY.** Really?

**HC.** Sometimes.

**SYDNEY.** Oh, HC.

**HC.** I love you.

**SYDNEY.** I...need you.

**HC.** It's nice to be needed. I need you.

**SYDNEY.** That feels nice.

**HC.** He said. He said. He said –

**SYDNEY.** Yes! He said, "Just resting my eyes."

**HC.** "Let's just say it'll be a picnic."

**SYDNEY.** "Yeah. Uh. Huh. Yeah. Really?"

**HC.** "Good and good for you."

| **SYDNEY.** | **HC.** |
|---|---|
| "Meet me at the Big Burn chairlift at two o'clock." | "Meet me at the Big Burn chairlift at two o'clock." |

*(The chairlift starts moving.)*

**SYDNEY.** It's moving!

**HC.** I need help! I don't know how to get off this thing. Dad helped me with this.

**SYDNEY.** I got you. Don't worry. I'm here. Boards up.

**HC.** Boards up.

> *(**SYDNEY** and **HC** raise their legs, "boards" facing the audience. **SYDNEY** takes hold of **HC**'s hand.)*

**SYDNEY.** Almost there.

**HC.** Okay.

**SYDNEY.** One.

**HC.** Two.

| **SYDNEY.** | **HC.** |
|---|---|
| Three. | Three. |

*(Blackout.)*

**End of Play**

# Reverse/Loop/Repeat

Steph Del Rosso

*REVERSE/LOOP/REPEAT* was first produced by Theater Masters in Aspen, Colorado from February 4 – 7, 2017. The performance was directed by Daisy Walker, with sets by R. Thomas Ward and lighting by Cooper Mulderry and R. Thomas Ward. The production stage manager was Mark C. Hoffner. The cast was as follows:

**WOMAN** . . . . . . . . . . . . . . . . . . . . . . . . . . . . . . . . . . . . . . . . . . . . . . . . Amy Honey
**MAN** . . . . . . . . . . . . . . . . . . . . . . . . . . . . . . . . . . . . . . . . . . . . . . . . . . . Dan Bosko

*REVERSE/LOOP/REPEAT* was subsequently produced by Theater Masters and Theater for the New City in New York City from May 2 – 6, 2017. The performance was directed by Daisy Walker, with sets by R. Thomas Ward and lights by Chris Thielking. The production stage manager was Mark C. Hoffner. The cast was as follows:

**WOMAN** . . . . . . . . . . . . . . . . . . . . . . . . . . . . . . . . . . . . . . . . Rebekah Brockman
**MAN** . . . . . . . . . . . . . . . . . . . . . . . . . . . . . . . . . . . . . . . . . . . . . . . . Ryan Barry

# CHARACTERS

**WOMAN**

**MAN**


# SETTING

A bedroom

A bar


# TIME

The recent past

The not-so-recent past

The deep past


# AUTHOR'S NOTES

**On transitions:**

Jumps in time are indicated by a (*).

The shifts should be fast – no pauses, no blackouts. Times blend into one another.

This play and these people move quickly.

**On set:**

Minimal. Spaces should be suggested and embodied in the language rather than furniture.

*(**WOMAN** sits. Maybe on a bed.)*
*(**MAN** sits beside her.)*
*(He takes her hand in his.)*

**MAN.** Hey.

**WOMAN.** Hey.

*(**MAN** takes her other hand in his.)*

**MAN.** I –

Wow, I didn't think this would be so hard

**WOMAN.** *(...)* It's okay

**MAN.** I –

*(**MAN** gets down on one knee.)*

**WOMAN.** *(!)* Oh my god

**MAN.** I wanted to ask you

**WOMAN.** *(!!)* Oh my god

**MAN.** Or

tell you

*(**MAN** gets down on both knees.)*

*(Wait a second...)*

I'm sorry – I'm just trying to find the / right

**WOMAN.** *(...!!)* It's okay, it's okay

**MAN.** The most comforta / ble

**WOMAN** *(...!)* Do whatever you need.

*(Micro beat.)*

**MAN.** I need to erase a quadrant of my life.

**WOMAN.** ...

**MAN.** I said I need to erase a quadrant of my life.

**WOMAN.** *(?)* Sorry

**MAN.** I'm gonna need some space

**WOMAN**. Like. Physical space?

**MAN**. Like:

    Things change. Things can lose their sheen.

**WOMAN**. *(Trying to laugh?)* I don't think I'm following

**MAN**. What I'm saying is: I can't picture myself with you in the future,

    And by that I mean this summer,

    And by that I mean in three months,

    And by that I mean in two weeks,

    And by that I mean tomorrow night.

**WOMAN**. *(...)* I'm free Sunday

**MAN**. I want to see other people.

**WOMAN**. *(...?)* Didn't you say you were erasing the whole quadrant

**MAN**. Well those were just words.

**WOMAN**. *(Trying!)* You always had a way with words!

**MAN**. *(Going with it.)* I'm a poet and I didn't know it!

**WOMAN**. *(Trying!)* The pen is mightier than the sword!

**MAN**. *(Over it.)* Yeah, I need to go

**WOMAN**. Can you wait?

**MAN**. But then I'll miss my chance, I mean my train, I mean – everything

**WOMAN**. I'll miss You

**MAN**. *(Nah.)* You'll just miss the idea of me

**WOMAN**. No I'll miss you-you

    You ordering Thai food at midnight

    You anxious at a crowded bar, toasting to Sam Cooke

**MAN**. *(Not remembering.)* What?

**WOMAN**. Please. Don't do this

**MAN**. That's just a thing people say

**WOMAN**. Please don't do this?

**MAN**. I've seen it on greeting cards and sides of buses

**WOMAN**. Who are you?

**MAN**. I'm getting antsy. I'm jumping out of my skin

**WOMAN.** Who the fuck are you?

**MAN.** I NEED TO GO

**WOMAN.** Where?

**MAN.** Away

**WOMAN.** Away where?

**MAN.** Not sure. Looks like the Wild West

**WOMAN.** Cowboys

**MAN.** Looks like Oz

**WOMAN.** Emeralds

**MAN.** Looks like the moon

**WOMAN.** Craters

**MAN.** Looks like my life without you

**WOMAN.** Is it sunny? Is it balmy? Is it tropical? Is it kinky? Is it low-maintenance? Is it emotional but not overemotional? Is it just-one-of-the-guys? Is she beautiful? Is this easy?

**MAN.** I'm losing service – I mean I'm on a really quiet bus – I mean I'll write you a letter – I mean a postcard – I mean a singing telegram – I mean I dropped my phone in the sink – I mean in the vodka – I mean in the wishing well – I mean I wish you well

**WOMAN.** Hang on hang on hang on please. This is serious, I promise it's serious:
I woke up with this hole on my knee. This big fat hole right on my knee where your hand used to go

**MAN.** Are you bleeding /

**WOMAN.** It feels like it /

**MAN.** Are you bleeding /

**WOMAN.** It feels like it but there's just this hole – you'd expect to see red blood cells muscle tissue bone but there's just this hole
So what am I supposed to do?

**MAN.** You'll be fine.

**WOMAN.** I don't want to be fine I want to be /

    *

**MAN.** Amazing

**WOMAN.** No way

**MAN.** You look amazing

**WOMAN.** I look tired

**MAN.** Nope

**WOMAN.** Bags under my eyes

**MAN.** Uh-uh

**WOMAN.** Hair's probably all / tangled

**MAN.** You look great

**WOMAN.** What time is it? Haven't checked my phone in /

**MAN.** Hours?

**WOMAN.** Days?

**MAN.** Weeks?

> *(Do they laugh? They definitely look out the window.)*

**WOMAN.** The sky's kind of orange-pink so

**MAN.** Sunrise?

**WOMAN.** Sunset?

**MAN.** *(A bit.)* Half past a freckle?

**WOMAN.** *(A bit.)* A quarter to fourteen?

**MAN.** Time to
Order Mexican

**WOMAN.** *(Try again.)* Thai

**MAN.** *(Here we go.)* Papaya salad!

**WOMAN.** And peanut sauce!

> *(The following is a game – **MAN** and **WOMAN** feed off of each other, giddy with all that they have in common and all that they're excited to do together.)*

**MAN.** Time to Learn Czech

**WOMAN.** And learn salsa!

**MAN.** And turn water into wine

**WOMAN.** And wine into whiskey

**MAN.** And write each other letters

**WOMAN.** And write each other songs

**MAN.** And climb Machu Picchu!

**WOMAN.** And see the Northern Lights!

**MAN.** And start a band?

**WOMAN.** And start a revolution

**MAN.** And save the planet

**WOMAN.** And save the children

**MAN.** And call our senators!

**WOMAN.** And call our parents more!

**MAN.** And grow a garden

**WOMAN.** And grow old.
Where'd you come from?

**MAN.** Down the road a ways.

**WOMAN.** I'll be washing my hands or waiting for my water to boil and I'll think, "Where'd you come from?"

**MAN.** Doesn't matter. Some place pre-you.

**WOMAN.** *(Faux-casual.)* Who else was uh there?

**MAN.** A redhead

**WOMAN.** She was a sculptor, right?

**MAN.** *(Wrong...)* Tap dancer

**WOMAN.** And then Charlotte

**MAN.** *(Wrong again...)* Andrea. Dental hygienist

**WOMAN.** And then the one with the sleeve tattoo. The waitress

**MAN.** *(Wrong again...)* She cut hair. But first, Bridget. With the freckles

**WOMAN.** She was a paralegal

**MAN.** *(Anddd wrong again...)* We were in high school. She'd sit on my shoulders at outdoor concerts

**WOMAN.** Thanks for the visual

**MAN.** Thanks for the memory lane trip

**WOMAN.** And you'd say the same things to them that you're saying to me right now

(**MAN** *looks at* **WOMAN**.)

**WOMAN.** And you'd look at them the way you're looking at me right now. I'm not accusing you I'm just /

**MAN.** Loss plus time divided by disdain equals disinterest

**WOMAN.** Insecurity divided by curiosity times obsession equals more insecurity

**MAN.** What about for you?

**WOMAN.** There were five or six. If I move fast enough they disappear

**MAN.** Let's open the windows, let's cook a feast
Let's do that thing where we don't worry or wound or fuck up or get sad!

**WOMAN.** Let's do that thing!

**MAN.** You know, when you're excited, your voice rises one octave. And your brown eyes get all glassy. And there's a single line in your brow. And when you truly think something is funny, your laugh is this silent, pulsing little heave. And you throw your head back. And you're all teeth

**WOMAN.** Oh yeah?

**MAN.** What time is it now

**WOMAN.** The point of no return

**MAN.** The point of /

*

**WOMAN.** My story is to try and impress you

**MAN.** The point of *my* story is to try and impress *you*

**WOMAN.** I think it's working

**MAN.** Yeah?

**WOMAN.** I hope it's working

**MAN.** I would call this Jittery Me

**WOMAN.** I would call this Animated Me

**MAN.** I would call this Totally Taken By You Me

**WOMAN.** Yeah I would call this Very Very Attracted To You Me

**MAN.** This is also Drunk Me

**WOMAN.** Oh this is Drunk Me, too

**MAN.** This is
Funny and Charming Me?

**WOMAN.** Yeah. This is Pleasantly Surprised Me

**MAN.** But I'm not sure how you'll feel about Tired and Pissed Off Me

**WOMAN.** I'm not sure how you'll feel about Indecisive Me

**MAN.** Self-Centered Me

**WOMAN.** Basket Case Me

**MAN.** I think I'll feel fine

**WOMAN.** You say that now, but /

**MAN.** I think I'll really feel fine

**WOMAN.** Yeah you say that now, but /

**MAN.** What do you want for round two?

**WOMAN.** Three

**MAN.** Four

**WOMAN.** I'll try the Molar Quaker, then the Toupee Faker

**MAN.** I'll go with the Elevator Wrecker, then the Mind Eraser

**WOMAN.** These sound like carnival rides

**MAN.** To carnival rides!

**WOMAN.** To speakeasies!

**MAN.** To Sam Cooke!

**WOMAN.** I think it's Otis!

**MAN.** I think this might be a sign

**WOMAN.** What's your sign?

**MAN.** Democrat – I mean Diplomat – I mean Conscientious Objector – I mean Taurus

**WOMAN.** I don't really believe in that shit

**MAN.** I like you

**WOMAN.** In this dim light you do, in this bourbon light you do

**MAN.** I just do

**WOMAN.** Later, much later, I'll cry my eyes out beside a dirty Chinese restaurant in a California suburb

**MAN.** Later, much later, I'll scream into a payphone in some tiny podunk town in South Dakota

**WOMAN.** And later, much later, you'll say that you're antsy, make me feel deficient, make me feel small

**MAN.** And later, much later, I'll find your hair in my shower drain, miss you, then paper over you with someone else

**WOMAN.** At a certain point I'll hate you a little

**MAN.** At a certain point I'll hate myself a little

**WOMAN.** At a certain point I'll sing this exact same song at a karaoke bar in Nashville, and kill it

**MAN.** At a certain point I'll ask you to get coffee and you'll decline

**WOMAN.** So. What now?

**MAN.** Well

> (**MAN** *puts his hand on* **WOMAN**'s *knee.*)
>
> (*Blackout.*)

**End of Play**

# Ron Don Jon Juan

Anna Fox

*RON DON JON JUAN* was first produced by Theater Masters in Aspen, Colorado from February 4 – 7, 2017. The performance was directed by Stephen Cedars, with sets by R. Thomas Ward and lighting by Cooper Mulderry and R. Thomas Ward. The production stage manager was Mark C. Hoffner. The cast was as follows:

**ELLERY** . . . . . . . . . . . . . . . . . . . . . . . . . . . . . . . . . . . . . . . . . . . Wendy Perkins
**RON** . . . . . . . . . . . . . . . . . . . . . . . . . . . . . . . . . . . . . . . . . . . . . Scott Elmore
**DON** . . . . . . . . . . . . . . . . . . . . . . . . . . . . . . . . . . . . . . . . . . . . Franz Alderfer
**JON** . . . . . . . . . . . . . . . . . . . . . . . . . . . . . . . . . . . . . . . . . . . Jason Cirkovic
**JUAN** . . . . . . . . . . . . . . . . . . . . . . . . . . . . . . . . . . . . . . . . . . Willie Moseley

*RON DON JON JUAN* was subsequently produced by Theater Masters and Theater for the New City in New York City from May 2 – 6, 2017. The performance was directed by Stephen Cedars, with sets by R. Thomas Ward and lights by Chris Thielking. The production stage manager was Mark C. Hoffner. The cast was as follows:

**ELLERY** . . . . . . . . . . . . . . . . . . . . . . . . . . . . . . . . . . . . . . . . . . . . . Joan Porter
**RON** . . . . . . . . . . . . . . . . . . . . . . . . . . . . . . . . . . . . . . . . . . . . . . Ryan Barry
**DON** . . . . . . . . . . . . . . . . . . . . . . . . . . . . . . . . . . . . . . . . . . Matthew Lawler
**JON** . . . . . . . . . . . . . . . . . . . . . . . . . . . . . . . . . . . . . . . . . . . . Will Manning
**JUAN** . . . . . . . . . . . . . . . . . . . . . . . . . . . . . . . . . . . . . . . . . Pietro Gonzalez

# CHARACTERS

**ELLERY B. JAMES HOFFMYER ELK GONZALEZ** – Eighties. White. Dying.

**RON JAMES** – Twenties. White. WWII soldier.

**DON HOFFMYER** – Forties. White. 1950s businessman.

**JON ELK** – Twenties. White. 1970s blonde surfer dude/air conditioner repairman.

**JUAN GONZALEZ** – Fifties. Mexican. Early 2000s poet.

*The male characters should all have singing/harmonizing abilities.

*(A stark hospital room. **ELLERY** lies on a cot with a pamphlet in front of her on the little tray where perhaps food should be, but is not. The back wall is vast and made of white scrim. She should look very small in a sea of sterile hospital. When the lights come up, **ELLERY** is mid-loneliness routine. She adjusts her bed up and down with a button; it makes noises. She looks around the room. She sips some water. She adjusts the bed again. She fumbles with the pamphlet. She presses the call button. She sips some water. She fumbles with the pamphlet. She presses the call button again and again and again.)*

**ELLERY**. I'm going to die.

*(Pause.)*

At least that's what they tell me.

*(She looks at the pamphlet.)*

"What to Expect When You're Expecting the End."

*(She opens the pamphlet.)*

Step One: Face it.

*(Pause. She faces it.)*

Okay.

Step Two: Seek guidance.

*(She looks for guidance.)*

*(She looks to the audience.)*

*(She gives up.)*

Step Three: Tell them you love them one more time before their brittle bones break and their souls ascend to a realm only imagined by those with still fully functioning prefrontal cortexes.

*(She puts the pamphlet down.)*

I suppose this was meant for the ones I'm supposed to seek guidance from. But they're not here.

*(She looks around.)*

Obviously.

*(She eyes the pamphlet.)*

I'm going to die and all I got was this lousy pamphlet.

*(Pause. She laughs. A little. She stops. She adjusts the bed.)*

*(To audience.)* I suppose if you have the time, maybe you'd like to hear a little story?

*(She waits for some sort of response, but doesn't care if she gets one or not.)*

A story about a young woman named Ellery Belinda Zarinsky. That's me.

Or at least it was.

Before my husbands.

All four of them.

*(Pause.)*

Say what you will, but I'm an independent woman.

Or at least I was…

*(She reads the pamphlet.)*

"Your hands will begin to feel cool. Your mind will start to wander."

*(She puts the pamphlet down.)*

As I was saying. What was I saying?

Once I had a dream that my four husbands were playing a game of four square.

And they wouldn't give me the ball…

Four square. Mind wandering. Dreams. Husbands.

Once I was a young woman named Ellery Belinda Zarinsky.

Now I'm an old woman named Ellery Belinda James Hoffmyer Elk Gonzalez.

No hyphens.

And soon I will be...

> *(She looks up toward some heavenly region. She looks back down. She forces a smile.)*

Well.

Let's be optimistic, shall we?!

Let's start with my life.

My names. My husbands.

The ironic rhyming tragicomedy that was:

Ron Don Jon Juan.

> **(ELLERY** *clicks the call button and the lights shift dramatically. A silhouette of* **RON** *appears in his army fatigues behind the scrim.)*

> *(Sings.)*

FIRST THERE WAS RON.

*(Speaking.)* Vital stats.

Nineteen years old.

From Alabama.

Had an awful accent.

One of those southern ones.

Those southern SOUTHERN ones.

But he was very, very handsome...

> *(He appears from behind the scrim.)*

**RON**. Say what's a pretty thing like you doing all alone?

**ELLERY**. Only I couldn't understand him because of his SOUTHERN accent. So I just looked at him all peeved.

> *(She makes a dramatic face.* **RON** *offers her a hand.)*

**RON.** Say. Would you like to get a bite to eat?

**ELLERY.** *(Reading from the pamphlet.)* "Your appetite will decrease. Your body will start to shut down."

**RON.** I'll take that as a yes.

> *(He offers her his hand. Only* **ELLERY** *cannot get out of bed.* **ELLERY** *smiles, touching his hand. Then he salutes her and "goes off to war." She watches him go.)*

**ELLERY.** *(To audience.)* Oh don't look so sad.

> *(Like she's telling the audience a big secret.)* People die. In fact. I believe that's the first thing I told you. "I'm going to die."

> *(She suddenly feels weary. She pushes the button.)*

Apparently others are dying at a more rapid rate however. Like fruit flies.

> *(She presses the button again.* **DON** *appears.)*

**DON.** The thing about fruit flies is that they mate like crazy. They mate like crazy because they know they're going to die, so why not make the most of life? I'm not sure if that's true, but I read somewhere... Where's my newspaper? How was your day dear? Did your feminine "fatigue" finally dissipate? Did you prepare dinner? I mean, "prepare" as in did you use the can opener to open the pickled beets, and the peas? I read somewhere that the can opener was invented in the nineteenth century. In the United States. I'm sure it was invented in 3000 BC by an oriental. Fruit flies also carry diseases. I wonder if they spread fly to fly... Are you even listening to me? Where are the beets? Where is the can opener? Where is my newspaper? I can't find a god damn thing in this god damn house!

**ELLERY.** And then there was Don...

> *(***DON** *picks up the pamphlet.)*

**DON.** Tell that mousy little cleaning lady to stop moving all my god damn things.

(**ELLERY** *snatches the pamphlet from him.*)

**ELLERY**. Then put your god damn things away Donald!

**DON**. Are you talking back to me?

**ELLERY**. *(Reading.)* "You may feel regret. A hollow feeling beneath your bones."

*(To audience.)* Maybe I should have killed him.

*(She presses the call button.)*

I'm kidding. He killed himself. Too much whiskey...and beets. Haha.

*(It's not actually funny.)*

Oh come on! I told you. People die. They die all the time. And people make promises they don't keep. And people laugh at things that aren't funny and people say things like, "I'll never love again, not after..." but then it's the summer of love and your air conditioner is broken and...

*(**JON** appears.)*

**JON**. Hey uh ma'am? You're looking awfully hot. I mean – uh – I mean – hah – uh. Temperature-wise, you know as in uh – yeah. Radical couch you've hot. I mean got. I mean – yeah.

**ELLERY**.
FIRST THERE WAS RON THEN THERE WAS DON
THEN THERE WAS –

**JON**. Jon. Yeah...Jon.

**ELLERY**. *(Reading from the pamphlet.)* "And what if you find yourself at the end before you really began?"

*(To **JON**.)* Ellery B. James Hoffmyer, but you can call me Ellery B.

**JON**. That's a mighty long name Miss Hoffmyer.

**ELLERY**. Ellery. I've been around the block so to speak.

*(**JON**'s eyes widen.)*

*(To audience.)* If this were modern times, I'd bet Jon would have created an internet dating profile saying

he was looking for an older lady, a "cougar" if you will. But at the time there was just me, him and a faulty air conditioner. I asked him if he wanted to make love to me on my "radical couch" and he said –

**JON.** Radical.

**ELLERY.** Then, somehow I woke up five years later from a strange dream. One where I married someone young enough to be my son and stupid enough to overdose on the painkillers I had started taking for my "older woman" back problems. The cougar outlived the cub.

> *(Pause.)*

> *(Reading from the pamphlet.)* "Perhaps you will want to sleep more than usual. Perhaps you will want to sleep forever."

>> *(She sighs. She tries to drink water. There is none left. She presses the call button.)*

>> *(Nothing happens.)*

>> *(She considers the pamphlet. She tries to read the Spanish on the back. She's bad at it.)*

Cuando tea. Te? Tea? Cuando tea enfrent-ass. Oh whatever. I should have learned Spanish. That's my one regret. Honestly.

> *(**JUAN** appears.)*

**JUAN.** Cuando te enfrentas el final.

Mirar a dios.

Mirar la luz.

No estas solo.

¿Has cerrado todas las puertas?

¿Has dicho adiós?

**ELLERY.** *(Suddenly reanimated. To audience.)* And then there was Juan.

*(To **JUAN**.)* Oh Juan. Your poetry is like music to my tired ears.

**JUAN.** I'm just reading the pamphlet, but in Spanish.

**ELLERY**. You are like my own private Pablo Neruda.
*(Like the white woman she is.)* Que romantico!

**JUAN**. Pablo Neruda was Chilean.
I'm Mexican.

**ELLERY**. I'm sorry. Please forgive me. I'm not as worldly as you.

**JUAN**. I always try to forgive you Ellery.

**ELLERY**. *(Reading/pronouncing it poorly.)* ¿Has dicho adiós?

**JUAN**. Have you said goodbye?

> (**ELLERY** *tries not to consider this and looks for something to distract herself with, but she's running out of options. She clutches the pamphlet like a lifesaver.)*

**ELLERY**. *(Reading.)* "You might start imagining things. You might talk to people who aren't there"

**JUAN**. Ellery?

**ELLERY**. *(Reading.)* "Your body is still here, but your spirit may have already left you."

**JUAN**. I'm concerned about you.

**ELLERY**. *(Reading.)* "Those who are concerned for you will be here to guide you through this process."

**JUAN**. I am here.

> (**ELLERY** *looks at him. She presses the button. He stays there. She presses it again. He stays. Again. He still stays. She breaks down. He goes to her.)*

**ELLERY**. I'm going to die.

**JUAN**. I know.

> *(They sit there for a moment. Then he starts to leave. During her speech the* **MEN** *all appear around her, like spirits, and possibly hum, underscoring her monologue.)*

**ELLERY**. Where are you going?
Juan?
Ron? Don? Jon?

How did I get here?

Did I ever really know myself? Why did I give up eating sugar? Maybe I should pray.

I'm not religious.

Juan prayed.

He wasn't religious either.

"Once a Catholic, always a Catholic," he'd say.

But he's not here!

No one is here I am alone.

I've always been alone.

And then,

Juan.

And then,

It was Thursday,

It was raining.

And silent and cold and the broken metal,

And the bits of brain on the pavement,

And I felt a feeling I had never felt before,

Like my insides were all falling out,

And I was ashamed.

Why am I telling you this?

At age seventy-three years old,

I was ashamed that I could love someone that much.

Had I never been in love before this?

Maybe I had just been entertaining ideas of men,

Who were supposed to "Fix me" and my air conditioner,

But this was different.

This was...

Juan used words to create meaning,

And I could barely describe what I had for breakfast.

You will "get over it,"

And you will "seek guidance" or "face it" or do whatever this god-awful stupid pamphlet tells you to do.

> *(She rips up the pamphlet and throws it on the ground.)*

But you never will.

There is never enough time,

And nothing is ever the same,

And that's what I –

> *(Suddenly, she speaks Spanish with an impeccable accent.)*

Mirar a dios.

Mirar la luz.

> *(She dies. As the **MEN** sing, the lights brighten and **ELLERY** opens her eyes. She gets out of bed and walks toward the light.)*

**RON, DON, JON & JUAN.**
FIRST THERE WAS RON THEN THERE WAS DON*
THEN THERE WAS JON
AND THEN THERE WAS JUAN
THEN YOU WERE GONE
LIFE DIDN'T GO ON
LIFE DIDN'T GO ON

> *(The **MEN** disappear.)*

> *(**JUAN** is the last one, lingering a bit longer and watching **ELLERY**.)*

> *(Then, **JUAN** exits.)*

> *(Now, it's just **ELLERY**. Alone. She looks toward the audience, at once peaceful and disturbed.)*

> *(Blackout.)*

**End of Play**

---

*The tune to this song was made up by the original director during rehearsals. You are encouraged to take your own creative license with it.

# Sink. Row. Nice!

Marvin González De León

*SINK. ROW. NICE!* was first produced by Theater Masters in Aspen, Colorado from February 4 – 7, 2017. The performance was directed by Daisy Walker, with sets by R. Thomas Ward and lighting by Cooper Mulderry and R. Thomas Ward. The production stage manager was Mark C. Hoffner. The cast was as follows:

**AMERICA** . . . . . . . . . . . . . . . . . . . . . . . . . . . . . . . . . . . . . . . . . . Ciara Morrison
**RUSSIA** . . . . . . . . . . . . . . . . . . . . . . . . . . . . . . . . . . . . . . . . . . . . Amy Honey
**EL SALVADOR** . . . . . . . . . . . . . . . . . . . . . . . . . . . . . . . . . . . Nakiri Gallagher

*SINK. ROW. NICE!* was subsequently produced by Theater Masters and Theater for the New City in New York City from May 2 – 6, 2017. The performance was directed by Daisy Walker, with sets by R. Thomas Ward and lights by Chris Thielking. The production stage manager was Mark C. Hoffner. The cast was as follows:

**AMERICA** . . . . . . . . . . . . . . . . . . . . . . . . . . . . . . . . . . . . . . . . . . Taylor Shurte
**RUSSIA** . . . . . . . . . . . . . . . . . . . . . . . . . . . . . . . . . . . . . . . . . . Rebecca White
**EL SALVADOR** . . . . . . . . . . . . . . . . . . . . . . . . . . . . . . . . . . . Alexandra Lemus

# CHARACTERS

**AMERICA** – Twenties. Female. Blond. A swimmer for the U.S. Women's Swim Team.

**RUSSIA** – Twenties. Female. Passable Russian. A swimmer for Russia's Women's Swim Team.

**EL SALVADOR** – Twenties. Female. Latina. A swimmer for El Salvador's Women's Swim Team.

# SETTING

Tokyo, Japan.

Completely clear set, except three black blocks for actors.
Nothing more. Nothing less.

# TIME

2020 Summer Olympics
(The XXXII Olympiad)

# AUTHOR'S NOTES

### Costumes
The swimmers wear national team warm-ups, parkas, swim caps, and goggles. America wears headphones – something like Beats by Dre.

### Punctuation
A ( / ) denotes where the next line of dialogue begins.

*(Lights up.* **AMERICA, RUSSIA,** *and* **SALVADOR**
*split the stage in even threes.)*

*(They dance.* **SALVADOR** *does the "sink" part of
"The Swim."* **RUSSIA** *does the "swimming" part
of "The Swim."* **AMERICA** *does "The Twist" as –)*

| **SALVADOR.** | **RUSSIA.** | **AMERICA.** |
|---|---|---|
| Sink. | | |
| | Row. | |
| | | Nice! |
| Sink. | | |
| | Row. | |
| | | Nice! |
| Sink. | | |
| | Row. | |
| | | Nice! |

**SALVADOR, RUSSIA & AMERICA.** SYNCHRONIZE!!

**AMERICA.** *(Bob Costas-esque.)* Ladies and gentlemen,
welcome to the thirty-second Olympiad from exotic
Tokyo, Japan. There's a *t*angible *t*enor of *t*ension in the
air *t*onight as the finest Women athletes in the world
prepare backstage to compete in the most grueling
swimming event of all – the 200M Butterfly!

> *(***SALVADOR, RUSSIA,** *and* **AMERICA** *do a
> transitional flourish –)*
>
> *(We hear Costa Rica's* national anthem as –)*
>
> *(***AMERICA** *and* **RUSSIA** *do the "sink" dance as –)*

---

*This is intentionally the wrong national anthem.

**85**

| SALVADOR. | RUSSIA. | AMERICA. |
|---|---|---|
| *(Frantic.)* | *(Whisper.)* | *(Whisper.)* |
| *Yo soy El Salvador.* We first compete in Olympics in 1968, but never win a medal. No one even knows we are here – I guess that's why they played Costa Rica's national anthem instead of ours!! I am just a little girl raised on a coffee farm – How the hell did I make the qualifying time?! I can't compete with these two! Russia?! They genetically engineer their athletes. Look at her! She looks like a werewolf! And, America? *¡Olvídalo!* They design their athletes in Cupertino and manufacture them in China – *¡Estoy jodida! (Beat.)* El Salvador means "The Savior." To him I pray. Because, I gonna SINK without divine intervention! *¡Chingado!* | Sink... Sink... Sink... Sink... Sink... Sink... Sink... Sink... Sink... Sink... Sink... Sink... Sink... Sink... Sink... Sink... Sink... Sink... Sink... Sink... Sink... Sink... Sink... Sink... Sink... Sink... Sink... Sink... Sink... Sink... | Sink... Sink... Sink... Sink... Sink... Sink... Sink... Sink... Sink... Sink... Sink... Sink... Sink... Sink... Sink... Sink... Sink... Sink... Sink... Sink... Sink... Sink... Sink... Sink... Sink... Sink... Sink... Sink... Sink... Sink... |

(**SALVADOR**, **RUSSIA**, *and* **AMERICA** *do a transitional flourish as –*)

(*We hear Russia's national anthem; then –*)

(**AMERICA** *and* **EL SALVADOR** *do the "swim" dance as –*)

| SALVADOR. | RUSSIA. | AMERICA. |
|---|---|---|
| *(Whisper.)* | *(Defiant.)* I am | *(Whisper.)* |
| Row... | Russia. I spit | Row... |
| Row... | on America | Row... |
| Row... | – imperialist | Row... |
| Row... | swine! Paw! | Row... |
| Row... | *(She spits.)* | Row... |
| Row... | I must defeat | Row... |
| Row... | her. If not, I | Row... |
| Row... | return to Russia | Row... |
| Row... | shamed woman. | Row... |
| Row... | I. Am. Bear! | Row... |
| Row... | And, I will eat | Row... |
| Row... | Bald Eagle for | Row... |
| Row... | breakfast! Even | Row... |
| Row... | though I am on | Row... |
| Row... | strict vegetarian | Row... |
| Row... | diet. As daughter | Row... |
| Row... | of steelworker, | Row... |
| Row... | I dreamed of | Row... |
| Row... | bringing hammer | Row... |
| Row... | down on Ms. | Row... |
| Row... | America! | Row... |
| Row... | *(She pulls a* | Row... |
| Row... | *picture of Putin* | Row... |
| Row... | *from her swimsuit* | Row... |
| Row... | *and kisses it.)* | Row... |
| Row... | I swim for | Row... |
| Row... | Putin! I swim for | Row... |
| Row... | mother Russia. I | Row... |
| Row... | swim with | |

| | | |
|---|---|---|
| Row... | strength of forty women! And, not because of mischievous performance-enhancing drugs – That is American lie! In Russia, you work hard, or life will crush you! That is why I row. Row. ROW!! | Row... |
| Row... | | Row... |
| Row... | | Row... |
| Row... | | Row... |
| Row... | | Row... |
| Row... | | Row... |
| Row... | | Row... |
| Row... | | Row... |
| Row... | | Row... |
| Row... | | Row... |
| Row... | | Row... |
| Row... | | Row... |

(**SALVADOR**, **RUSSIA**, *and* **AMERICA** *do a transitional flourish as –)*

*(We hear the U.S. national anthem; then –)*

(**SALVADOR** *and* **RUSSIA** *do "The Twist" as –)*

| SALVADOR. | RUSSIA. | AMERICA. |
|---|---|---|
| *(Whisper.)* | *(Whisper.)* | *(Confidently.)* I am America. I look in the mirror – I see the face of a winner. I was born in a mall in Houston, Texas next to the food court! NICE! I am Duncan MacLeod of Clan MacLeod – the Highlander! Get in my way; I'll chop off your fucking head, because in the end THERE CAN BE ONLY ONE! Wha-cha! I float like a butterfly, but sting like a bee. |
| Nice! | Nice! | |
| Nice! | Nice! | |
| Nice! | Nice! | |
| Nice! | Nice! | |
| Nice! | Nice! | |
| Nice! | Nice! | |
| Nice! | Nice! | |
| Nice! | Nice! | |
| Nice! | Nice! | |
| Nice! | Nice! | |
| Nice! | Nice! | |
| Nice! | Nice! | |
| Nice! | Nice! | |
| Nice! | Nice! | |

| | | |
|---|---|---|
| Nice! | Nice! | I am super-fly-TNT! |
| Nice! | Nice! | I pity the fool who |
| Nice! | Nice! | steps up to me! |
| Nice! | Nice! | So, listen up – the |
| Nice! | Nice! | woman swimming |
| Nice! | Nicc! | against the stream |
| Nice! | Nice! | knows the strength of |
| Nice! | Nice! | it. I am the stream! |
| Nice! | Nice! | Know my strength, |
| | | bitches!! |

(**SALVADOR**, **RUSSIA**, *and* **AMERICA** *do a transitional flourish as –*)

(*We hear a loud whistle –*)

**RUSSIA.** (*Russian Bob Costas-esque.*) We can only surmise what goes on in these Women's heads as they prepare for what will be the most grueling test of their lives.

(**AMERICA** *and* **RUSSIA** *do the "Electric Slide" as –*)

| SALVADOR. | RUSSIA. | AMERICA. |
|---|---|---|
| Before a race, / I think of the patron saint of athletes – San Sebastián. / Who was tied to a tree and shot with | ...You're not gonna win... | |
| | | ...You're a loser! |
| arrows / through the neck, and | ...You're... | ...You're... |
| pray / for a less asphyxiating | ...A | ...A |
| fate! / | ...Loser! | ...Loser! |

(**SALVADOR** *and* **AMERICA** *do the "Electric Slide" as –*)

| SALVADOR. | RUSSIA. | AMERICA. |
|---|---|---|
|  | Before race, I think of Grand |  |
| ...You're no duchess | Duchess / Anastasia | ...You're no duchess. |
| ...You're trash... | Nikoleavna! / I wish to escape captivity, too. Uncertainty fuels my drive. | ...You're trash... |
| ...Glorious... ... | / If I am victor, will it aid my obscurity, or add to my | ...Glorious... ... |
| ...Trash! | ostentation? / | ...Trash! |

>   (**SALVADOR** *and* **RUSSIA** *do the "Electric Slide"*
>   *as –)*

**AMERICA.** Before a race, I pray to no god but myself, and
rock out to Metallica! BAM!!

>   (**AMERICA** *puts on her headphones as –)*
>
>   *(We hear heavy metal\* turned up to eleven!)*
>
>   *(The swimmers head-bang for a hot minute;
>   then –)*
>
>   (**SALVADOR, RUSSIA,** *and* **AMERICA** *transitional
>   flourish and dance; then –)*

| SALVADOR. | RUSSIA. | AMERICA. |
|---|---|---|
| Sink. |  |  |
|  | Row. |  |
|  |  | Nice! |
| Sink. |  |  |
|  | Row. |  |

---

\*A license to produce *Sink. Row. Nice!* does not include a performance
license for any third-party or copyrighted music. Licensees should create
an original composition or use music in the public domain. For further
information, please see Music Use Note on page 3.

> Nice!

Sink.

> Row.

> Nice!

**SALVADOR.** *(Salvadoreño Bob Costas-esque.)* Here come the swimmers. Look at them. The top echelon of human athleticism!

> *(The **SWIMMERS** take off their warms-ups.)*

**SALVADOR, RUSSIA & AMERICA.** Take your position!

> *(The **SWIMMERS** take their swimmer stances as –)*

**AMERICA.** I am a dolphin!

**RUSSIA.** I am Dolph Lundgren!

**SALVADOR.** I am dolphin-itely not going to win!

**SALVADOR, RUSSIA & AMERICA.** Oh, no. There's the countdown.

| **SALVADOR.** | **RUSSIA.** | **AMERICA.** |
|---|---|---|
| *Tres. Dos. Uno.* | Три. Два. Один. | Three. Two. One. |

**SALVADOR, RUSSIA & AMERICA.** Tweeeeeeeeettttt!! And, they're off!!

> *(The **SWIMMERS** jump off the platforms and mimic that weird-fluid-dolphin-thing Olympic swimmers do at the beginning of a race; then –)*
>
> *(They start doing that butterfly-stroke motion, like, way-intensely –)*

**AMERICA.** *(Confident.)* I am fluid, formless, and aqueous. My body conforms to the motion of the oceans, like the swell of a tsunami or a sperm cell charging toward fertilization!

**RUSSIA.** *(Determined.)* I am hammerhead shark – the bulldozer of the sea! I come for you, Ms. America.

> *(**SALVADOR**, for some reason, starts flapping like a bird.)*

**SALVADOR.** *(Frantic.)* You're flapping like dove?! What's wrong with you? You're in water. Not air. Think of a marine lifeform – you idiot! A dove drowns in water! You are a fish!!

> (**SALVADOR** *resumes the butterfly stroke, along with* **RUSSIA** *and* **AMERICA** *as –*)

**RUSSIA.** *(Russian Bob Costas-esque.)* Wow! Look at them fillet the water! Amazing! Looks like America has pulled in front, but Russia follows close behind!

**AMERICA.** I am definitely the sperm that fertilizes the egg! Look at me stroke. And stroke. And stoke! With purpose. With determination. I'm a machine! Well-greased and ready to fuckin' murder all y'all!!

**RUSSIA.** Look at her. Smug little suka! Ha! I call you suka, 'cause you are! Pizda! Suka! And, loser to Russia!

**SALVADOR.** Breathe! Look ahead! You come from a wonderful country whose chief export is coffee! The bean that fuels the world! Let that bean fuel you to victory!!

**AMERICA.** *(Bob Costas-esque.)* Our swimmers have come to the end of the first lap –

> (*The* **SWIMMERS** *do that weird-fluid-dolphin-thing swimmers do as they transition between laps –*)

(*Bob Costas-esque.*) America leads the pack, Russia a close second, and, the surprise contender, El Salvador, coming up the rear!

**SALVADOR.** I'm coming up your rear! Ha hahahahah!

> (*Chokes/coughs.*)

Oh, shit! Swallowed some water!

**RUSSIA & AMERICA.** *(Bob Costas-esque.)* But, it looks like El Salvador is falling behind!

**SALVADOR.** *(Dreamy underwater voice.)* Shit! What am I doing here?! I'm sinking! Why can't we get along? Whaawhaa... Blub... Blub... Why. Must. We. Compete...

> (**SALVADOR** *is sinking. It's drastic and surreal and tragic.*)

>     *(But, in the middle of it all, a fantasy –)*

**SALVADOR, RUSSIA & AMERICA.** *(Dreamy underwater voice.)*
Why can't we...

| SALVADOR. | RUSSIA. | AMERICA. |
|---|---|---|
| Sink. | | |
| | Row. | |
| | | Nice! |
| Sink. | | |
| | Row. | |
| | | Nice! |
| Sink. | | |
| | Row. | |
| | | Nice! |

**SALVADOR, RUSSIA & AMERICA.** SYNCHRONIZE!!

>     *(Lights change.)*

>     *(We hear that famous section of Tchaikovsky's "Waltz of the Flowers" as they hum along and –)*

>     *(***SALVADOR, RUSSIA,*** *and* ***AMERICA*** *engage in a synchronized swimming routine. This dance can be as simple or elaborate as necessary.)*

>     *(They do the full range of synchronized swimming dances, from the Crane, the Knight, the Flamingo; that weird one where they make their arms look like the Loch Ness Monster. They do a maneuver where* ***SALVADOR*** *is in the middle and* ***AMERICA*** *and* ***RUSSIA*** *circle around her; arms in, arms out. The dance goes on, until they lift* ***SALVADOR*** *in a plank maneuver and she makes a swim motion as they twirl her around. This can last as long as you want it to, but –)*

>     *(The swimmers must hum "Waltz of the Flowers" the whole time, thusly –)*

DA DA DA DA DUM DUM DUM DUM
DO DO DO

DA DA DA DUM DUM
DO DO DO
DA DA DA DUM DUM
DO DO DO
DUM DUM DA DA DUM DADA DUM
DUM DUM DUM DUM DA DAH DUM
DUM DUM DUM DUM DA DUM DA DUM
DUM DUM DUM DUM DA DAH DUM
DUM DUM DUM DUM DA DAH DA DUM!

> *(...Or more or less an approximation of that.)*

> *(But, then –)*

> *(Back to the race – an arresting transition –)*

**RUSSIA.** *(Bob Costas-esque.)* What a dramatic race! Mere yards from the finish, and it's any woman's game!

**AMERICA.** Ahhhh! MY ARM!! MY ARM!!!

> *(One of **AMERICA**'s arms comes out of the socket and is rendered useless.)*

> *(**AMERICA** swims on determinedly with her bad arm hanging limply.)*

**RUSSIA.** The hammerhead can smell blood!

**SALVADOR.** C'mon! Swim, motherfucker!! Flap your wings!!

> *(**SALVADOR** starts to flap like a dove.)*

Jesus – lift me to victory!

> *(**SALVADOR** flaps furiously.)*

> *(**RUSSIA** and **AMERICA** stroke violently –)*

I'm imbued with the spirit!

**RUSSIA.** I'm hot on your scent!

**AMERICA.** I am flailing and floundering!! But, I can't lose!! I'm America – I always win!!

> *(The **SWIMMERS** do their thing – in their own way – with an unmatched gumption.)*

**SALVADOR.** *(Bob Costas-esque.)* Ladies and gentlemen, it's a photo finish at the end with Russia with the gold, America with the silver, and El Salvador with the bronze!

*(SALVADOR, RUSSIA, and AMERICA do a transitional flourish; then –)*

*(The SWIMMERS clap and cheer as though they were the audience.)*

*(The SWIMMERS gather –)*

*(A tableau – RUSSIA center, tallest; then AMERICA; then SALVADOR – on the left – kneels – all on different planes.)*

I am third in the world, but first in my country. *Gracias, Jesus. El señor está conmigo.*

AMERICA. My left arm is useless. It'll hang from my body like a sock full of nickels until the day I die. But, know what? ...I got endorsement deals! I'll be on Wheaties boxes and shit! The one-armed champ! Ahhh! The sweet taste of immortality!

*(RUSSIA stares at the picture of Putin.)*

RUSSIA. Putin won't approve. Yes, I win. But, I lose. Victory against broken woman is no real victory. I will never escape captivity. Putin won't approve.

*(They pull their metals out of their suits and put them around their necks as –)*

*(We hear uproarious applause. They stare out with pride and fear in their eyes.)*

| SALVADOR. | RUSSIA. | AMERICA. |
|---|---|---|
| Sink. | | |
| | Row. | |
| | | Nice! |
| Sink. | | |
| | Row. | |
| | | Nice! |
| Sink. | | |
| | Row. | |
| | | Nice! |

**SALVADOR, RUSSIA & AMERICA.** SYNCHRONIZE!!

> *(We hear/see the flashing of cameras as the uproarious applause continues.)*
>
> *(They bite into their metals, each making a face like a strange Greek mask.)*
>
> *(Blackout.)*

**End of Play**

# Sway

Kristen Field

*SWAY* was first produced by Theater Masters in Aspen, Colorado from February 4 – 7, 2017. The performance was directed by Stephen Cedars, with sets by R. Thomas Ward and lighting by Cooper Mulderry and R. Thomas Ward. The production stage manager was Mark C. Hoffner. The cast was as follows:

**DAVE** . . . . . . . . . . . . . . . . . . . . . . . . . . . . . . . . . . . . . . . . . . . . . . . . . Franz Alderfer

**MATT** . . . . . . . . . . . . . . . . . . . . . . . . . . . . . . . . . . . . . . . . . . . . . . . . . Ryan Honey

**BEC** . . . . . . . . . . . . . . . . . . . . . . . . . . . . . . . . . . . . . . . . . . . . . . . . . Lisa Langer

**RACHEL** . . . . . . . . . . . . . . . . . . . . . . . . . . . . . . . . . . . . . . . . . . . . . Emily Henley

**FIONA** . . . . . . . . . . . . . . . . . . . . . . . . . . . . . . . . . . . . . . . . . Barbara Bloemsma

*SWAY* was subsequently produced by Theater Masters and Theater for the New City in New York City from May 2 – 6, 2017. The performance was directed by Stephen Cedars, with sets by R. Thomas Ward and lights by Chris Thielking. The production stage manager was Mark C. Hoffner. The cast was as follows:

**DAVE** . . . . . . . . . . . . . . . . . . . . . . . . . . . . . . . . . . . . . . . . . . . . . . Matthew Lawler

**MATT** . . . . . . . . . . . . . . . . . . . . . . . . . . . . . . . . . . . . . . . . . . . . . . Will Manning

**BEC** . . . . . . . . . . . . . . . . . . . . . . . . . . . . . . . . . . . . . . . . . . . . . . . . Lisa Langer

**RACHEL** . . . . . . . . . . . . . . . . . . . . . . . . . . . . . . . . . . . . . . . . . . . Taylor Shurte

**FIONA** . . . . . . . . . . . . . . . . . . . . . . . . . . . . . . . . . . . . . . . . . . . Rebecca White

# CHARACTERS

**DAVE** – The host of a radio show. Not slim. Not young. Still charming.

**MATT** – One of Dave's co-hosts. A scraggly goatee has taken up residence on his chin. Shining eyes, but not in a good way. Adorably naive.

**BEC** – Dave's other co-host. Not young, but has to play at being young. Dying inside. A woman at the end of her rope who doesn't care that she's about to fall.

**RACHEL** – An actress in her thirties. Gorgeous. A warm smile paired with a closed-off expression.

**FEMALE CALLER** – A college-aged student.


# SETTING

A recording booth at a radio station.


# TIME

Early morning. Today.

*(Black nothingness. Before the lights go up, we hear a female voice – a voice that would be called shrill by many.)*

**FEMALE CALLER.** *(Voice-over.)* Oh, you're too sweet! But honestly. That woman probably looked like a troll – she really is insane for turning you down.

*(The lights go up sometime during* **DAVE**'s *following response, and we see the three* **HOSTS** *sitting side by side at the recording table and* **RACHEL** *sitting slightly off to the side, waiting.)*

**DAVE.** Well, she actually *was* an attractive woman – getting on, but she'd put in an effort, and there's something really sexy about that kind of desperation, you know?

**BEC.** *(Not even sure herself whether she's being serious.)* Of course. Nothing sexier than a woman with no other options. You should learn that now while you're still in your youth, Cindy.

**DAVE.** *(With an underlying antagonism to his words.)* Hey now, no need to tell a fellow woman what she needs to think!

**BEC.** I wouldn't dare. What's the point?

**DAVE.** Bec, you're a riot. Anyway, Cindy, we have a real treat for you and the rest of our listeners this morning because Rachel Ware is with us today to talk about this new play that she's in.

**FEMALE CALLER.** Rachel Ware? I don't really –

**DAVE.** Well, *technically* she's a theatre actress, but you probably know her from the Lexus ad she stars in. Matt, are you just jumping out of your pants with Rachel mere feet away from you?

MATT. I think that's a bit of an understatement, Dave, but *something's* certainly happening in the vicinity of my pants.

> (**DAVE** *chuckles, a manly chuckle, while* **BEC** *elicits some sort of sharp laugh, like she's literally squeezing it out of her lungs.*)

DAVE. I could watch that ad for *hours*, no question. Anyway, thanks for calling in, Cindy, and Rachel, thanks for being with us this morning. Great to have you here.

> (*When* **DAVE** *finally addresses her,* **RACHEL** *scoots toward the table in her swivel chair.*)

RACHEL. Pleasure to be here.

DAVE. So, tell us, do you have any idea of the effect you're having on the male population with this ad?

RACHEL. (*Laughing like she's not sure whether she should be horrified.*) Yes – yes I have heard the buzz. It's completely flattering, really, but I try my best to stay away from online comments about it – what people post on the YouTube clips of the ad, stuff like that.

DAVE. What? That's insane!

RACHEL. Well I just know the probability of there being something upsetting there, mixed in with – all the other comments. I just don't want to risk it.

DAVE. Risk what! I promise you, men are absolutely smitten. And that's no surprise at all with your *stunning* figure. And that face. It could launch a thousand ships, as they say.

RACHEL. (*Possibly dripping with sarcasm. Possibly buying into this game.*) Well, that's certainly lovely to hear. Wouldn't want to have a face that *couldn't* start a war.

BEC. I have to jump in and say that Matt's been caught just staring, mesmerised by this ad. It's actually quite embarrassing.

MATT. Come on, can you blame me? I mean, that sashay! I'm sure I'm not the only one.

**RACHEL.** You're certainly not. I got approached last night in the supermarket by a man who told me that I was his free pass with his wife.

| **BEC.** | **MATT.** |
|---|---|
| Really? What a world we live in. | But did you go home with him?? |

**DAVE.** It certainly must be wonderful for you, getting all that attention.

**RACHEL.** Well, it is and it isn't. I mean, I'm more than happy to put up with it because – well, with theatre – it's great, but if you want to make a name for yourself the stage probably isn't the place to do it.

**BEC.** Nope, to do *that* you need a tight-fitting dress and a role in a Lexus commercial.

**RACHEL.** *(Turning to* **BEC** *with restrained ire.)* Look, it's gotten me a supporting role in an indie film that starts shooting next month, so. Yeah. It's kind of worth it.

**BEC.** *(Mocking. And almost disbelieving.)* Kind of.

**DAVE.** *(To* **RACHEL**.*)* Don't worry, Bec just doesn't have the same appreciation for your skill set that we do. So, tell us, are you seeing anyone right now?

**RACHEL.** Sorry?

**BEC.** Dave really needs to learn some manners.

**DAVE.** Come on.

**BEC.** But I think he's trying to glean how available you are at the moment.

**RACHEL.** *(Trying not to let the unexpectedness of this derail the interview.)* Well, if you have a wife, Dave, I hope she's not listening! But unfortunately I am taken.

| **DAVE.** | **MATT.** |
|---|---|
| Nope, I'm free as a bird. | Rats! And there's nothing we could do to convince you to free yourself up? |

**RACHEL.** *(With as much lightness as she can muster.)* No! No, I'm afraid we're quite happy together. Sorry to disappoint you both, though!

DAVE. Well, if anything changes, you let us know.

BEC. Yes, *do* let us all know. Send us a subliminal message in the next installment of your epic journey as the struggling actress-slash-Lexus saleswoman.

RACHEL. *What* is your problem? Please tell me. Because I'd hate to leave here having *offended* you in some way.

DAVE. Don't worry about Bec – she finds a reason to hate everyone around her.

RACHEL. Sounds like my partner.

BEC. *(With a casual shrewdness.)* You mean your boyfriend?

> *(RACHEL says nothing, lost in indecision. BEC realizes exactly what she's done. DAVE is beginning to catch on, but MATT is clueless.)*

MATT. Just imagine actually doing it with this goddess. *(Almost despondent.)* What a lucky guy.

> *(RACHEL swallows, hoping she can still hold on to what this opportunity was meant to be.)*

DAVE. Is it a guy?

> *(Another beat. BEC is paralyzed, either with regret or anticipation. And then RACHEL snaps.)*

RACHEL. No, actually. I'm – seeing a woman. Have always seen women, actually. Never been with a man. Don't care to change that.

DAVE. Well, that's a bit rash, don't you think? Ruling out a whole gender?

RACHEL. Haven't you done just that?

MATT. I have to say, I'm definitely on board with this. If you're gonna ignore an entire gender it should definitely be men, right? Because women are amazing. Who wouldn't want to bang them?

DAVE. You do have a point there.

BEC. I actually don't know how I've put up with you two for so long.

RACHEL. I don't, either. But it's *kind* of your own fault that you've ended up here, isn't it? And it's not like you came to my rescue when I was propositioned on live radio a second ago.

BEC. Was I *meant* to? I mean after listening to you whine about how much of a toll it takes on you to star in a nationwide commercial and deal with the *adoration* people *lay down at your feet* I was meant to come to your *rescue*?

> (**DAVE** *clears his throat, getting ready to salvage this situation.*)

MATT. *(To* **RACHEL**, *indicating* **BEC**.*)* Are you coming on to *her*? Because I really don't see how that's any better than us "propositioning" you on the air. You still have a girlfriend. Unless you're in an open relationship? Is *she* into guys? That would honestly make my whole year.

RACHEL. Okay. First of all: I was not trying to hit on your co-host. I'm actually wondering how you could have possibly *ever* been with *anyone* if that's what your idea of flirting is. But your co-host is a bitch. And my girlfriend is not into men. And I'm really starting to see what she was trying to get at, going on about visibility and self-worth over the past five years.

BEC. *(To* **RACHEL**.*)* You're like a human *Jezebel* article, aren't you?

DAVE. It's a plague now, Matt. Every promising woman falling prey to these sapphic spells.

BEC. Will you *please* shut up before I actually slap you?

RACHEL. *(Almost under her breath.) You're* a human *Jezebel* article.

DAVE. Sweetie, I would *love* to see that.

BEC. Don't tempt me.

DAVE. So many empty threats. So little time until we go to commercial.

RACHEL. This is a total nightmare.

BEC. A nightmare? Really?

**DAVE.** A *nightmare* would be me *actually* hitting Bec. Not Bec *threatening* to hit me. In jest.

**BEC.** You really want to test that assumption?

**MATT.** Guys! Guys, come on. This is nothing worth throwing punches over.

**RACHEL.** Easy for you to say.

**BEC.** Come on, don't pretend this isn't making you wet, getting your activist on and spouting vitriol at these two pathetic losers.

**RACHEL.** I – you – really just said that, didn't you?

> *(Struggling to grasp something concrete.)*

And I actually outed myself. On a radio show. After being torn apart like a piece of meat.

**DAVE.** Hey, if you're feeling any regret, it's never too late to switch teams.

**RACHEL.** *(No more grace left to hold on to.)* I DO NOT WANT TO FUCK YOU.

**DAVE.** Well, we've got to take a quick break now, but we'll be back to talk to Rachel about her play and the wonderful sway of her hips!

> *(**DAVE** presses a button to send them to commercial.)*

**BEC.** *(To **RACHEL**, with a disturbingly calm air.)* You've really got to get it together. Like we're not meant to swear at all on the air.

**DAVE.** Come on, this is *gold*. After seeing the buzz this stirs up I bet you anything the station isn't even going to *mention* the f-bomb Rachel just dropped.

**MATT.** *(To **RACHEL**, an attempt at a congratulatory, supportive gesture.)* Kaboom!

**RACHEL.** *(Almost catatonic.)* What the fuck have I done.

**BEC.** Probably gotten yourself a whole new legion of fans, I'm guessing. People love the lesbians.

**MATT.** *(Totally sincere.)* They really do.

RACHEL. No I just – I thought her – the jealousy – was all some stupid manipulation. Trying to make me feel guilty for working.

> (**DAVE** *opens some chips. Starts eating. Offers some to* **MATT.***)*

BEC. And that's another terrible weight the world has placed on your shoulders?

RACHEL. Yes. Maybe. I don't know. But she was right. And now I just – I don't know how I'm going to go back to that. To her. After all of this.

DAVE. *(With his mouth full.)* Come on, your manager is gonna be sending us flowers and chocolate tomorrow for dragging this out of you.

RACHEL. It – it was my choice.

> *(A beat.)*

Wasn't it?

BEC. You tell me. I don't know half the time why I do what I do. Why I'm still here.

DAVE. Because you don't have any better options?

BEC. That's probably it.

MATT. *(To* **RACHEL,** *an almost-whisper.)* But like...you've *never* been with a guy? Not ever?

> *(The outrage/fear that* **RACHEL** *has been trying to quell since her last line explodes.)*

RACHEL. I thought the world was beyond this! That I was out of its reach being a small-time actress with no real success to my name I mean it wasn't even a *career* move to stay closeted because it wasn't even *necessary* I mean NO ONE CARED, YOU KNOW? But then this fucking ad came along and what kind of dipshit says no to a car commercial? I am not a dipshit. But I am a coward because I was totally content to just go along doing my own thing and accepting people's obsessions with my fucking hair and fucking dress and fucking smile and *fucking relationship status* as part and parcel of this chaos. But nope it was much more than that it was *so much fucking more* because people aren't just saying these things *they really want to fuck me* and like what does that even mean? What does that make me? And my relationship what does it do to that when I wanted nothing more than to hide it from people as insignificant as the fucking audience at a fucking adaptation of Ovid's *Metamorphoses*.

*(A beat. She breathes.)*

I was fucking terrified and I thought that made me crazy. But it didn't.

*(A beat. An unbearably heavy silence. Like we have to move toward laughter or tears or we'll suffocate in the liminality of the moment.)*

BEC. You sound pretty crazy to me. But what would I know?

*(Another beat. DAVE keeps eating chips. MATT is completely enthralled.)*

RACHEL. *(On the edge. Of something.)* Then where do you go from here? Knowing this? Knowing this is what you have to work with and this is what the world will take from you without a second thought?

BEC. You know – maybe the world does take and take and take from you – even from people like you – but you know what else? You're here. To promote a play. And a movie. And a commercial. Maybe just take a deep breath and recognize that. For one second. You're here.

*(A beat. Another breath.)*

RACHEL. *(Shell-shocked.)* Yeah. We're both here.

*(DAVE brings them back from commercial. A grand, sweeping gesture.)*

DAVE. And we're back.

*(Black.)*

**End of Play**